Advanced Java Programming: Build Robust Applications with Ease

A Complete Guide to Mastering Java for Complex Projects

BOOZMAN RICHARD

BOOKER BLUNT

Table of Content

TABLE OF CONTENTS

INTRODUCTION 6

Mastering Java for Complex Projects 6

Chapter 1 13

Introduction to Advanced Java Programming 13

Chapter 2 21

Java Language Basics Refresher..21

Chapter 3 33

Object-Oriented Programming in Depth....................................33

Chapter 4 48

Exception Handling and Debugging 48

Chapter 5 59

Working with Collections in Java..59

Chapter 6 72

Concurrency and Multithreading 72

Chapter 7 84

Java Streams and Lambda Expressions 84

Chapter 8 96

Java Memory Management and Garbage Collection 96

Chapter 9 106

Building Robust Applications with Design Patterns............... 106

Chapter 10 122

Java I/O and File Handling 122

Chapter 11 138

Networking and Sockets in Java 138

Chapter 12 154

Database Connectivity with JDBC 154

Chapter 13 171

Java Web Development Overview 171

Chapter 14 185

Spring Framework Basics 185

Chapter 15 198

Advanced Spring Framework 198

Chapter 16 214

JavaFX for Building Desktop Applications 214

Chapter 17 227

Testing Java Applications 227

Chapter 18 238

Dependency Management with Maven and Gradle 238

Chapter 19 251

Java for Cloud Development 251

Chapter 20 261

Microservices Architecture with Java 261

Chapter 21 274

Security in Java Applications 274

Chapter 22 287

Java for Big Data and Hadoop 287

Chapter 23 300

Java for Mobile Development (Android Basics) 300

Chapter 24: Reactive Programming with Java 304

Chapter 25 317

Performance Optimization and Profiling in Java......................317

Chapter 26..327

Java in the Internet of Things (IoT) 327

Chapter 27..339

Future of Java and Emerging Trends 339

INTRODUCTION

Mastering Java for Complex Projects

Welcome to **"Mastering Java for Complex Projects"**, a comprehensive guide designed to take you on a journey through the world of Java programming, from foundational concepts to advanced topics, equipping you with the skills necessary to develop sophisticated applications for today's dynamic technology landscape.

Java is one of the most widely used and enduring programming languages. It has consistently been a top choice for developers because of its robustness, scalability, security, and platform independence. Over the years, Java has evolved and adapted to meet the demands of modern software development, from web applications and mobile solutions to cloud-native systems and big data processing. This book will empower you to not only understand the intricacies of Java but also to leverage it in building complex systems that address real-world problems.

Whether you are a seasoned Java developer or someone new to the language, this book will guide you through the full spectrum of Java development. We have structured this book with both beginners and experienced developers in mind, providing clear explanations, practical examples, and insightful tips that will help you grasp even the most advanced topics.

Why Java for Complex Projects?

Java's versatility and long history of stability make it an ideal choice for developing complex and large-scale applications. As a developer, you will encounter numerous scenarios in your career that require the use of Java for building intricate systems, from enterprise-level applications to cloud-native microservices. Java's **object-oriented design**, **multithreading capabilities**, **rich standard library**, and **large ecosystem of frameworks and tools** all contribute to its success in handling demanding projects.

But as software systems become more complex, understanding Java alone is not enough. To build robust applications, you need to familiarize yourself with various **design patterns**, **architectural concepts**, and **emerging technologies**. This book is focused not only on improving your proficiency in Java, but also on equipping you with the ability to design, develop, and deploy high-performance applications in modern environments.

What You Will Learn in This Book

This book is divided into 27 chapters, each focusing on different aspects of Java programming and real-world application development. The following key topics will be covered in detail:

1. **Core Java Concepts**: We begin with a solid foundation of Java's syntax, object-oriented principles, and essential libraries. You'll gain a thorough understanding of data structures, algorithms, and memory management in Java.

2. **Object-Oriented Programming (OOP)**: Java's object-oriented nature is one of its most powerful features. You will learn advanced techniques of OOP, such as inheritance, polymorphism, and encapsulation, and apply them in real-world scenarios.

3. **Concurrency and Multithreading**: Java's built-in support for multithreading allows developers to efficiently handle parallel tasks. You will learn about thread management, synchronization, and concurrent programming techniques.

4. **Java in the Cloud**: Modern applications require scalability and flexibility, and Java's role in **cloud computing** has grown substantially. This book introduces you to **Java for cloud-native development**, covering tools like **Spring Boot**, **Docker**, and **Kubernetes** to help you deploy Java applications in cloud environments.

5. **Big Data and Hadoop**: With the rise of large-scale data processing, Java plays a crucial role in handling **Big Data**. We'll explore how Java interfaces with frameworks like **Hadoop** and **Apache Spark** to process and analyze massive datasets.

6. **Security in Java**: Security is a primary concern in modern applications. We'll discuss common security vulnerabilities like **SQL Injection** and **XSS**, and teach you how to implement secure coding practices, including **OAuth2** authentication and **encryption techniques**.

7. **Reactive Programming**: As applications move toward real-time, non-blocking operations, **reactive programming** has become a critical skill. This book introduces **Project Reactor** and **RxJava**, guiding you to write **asynchronous** and **event-driven** applications.

8. **IoT with Java**: Java is a popular choice for **Internet of Things (IoT)** applications. Learn how to connect sensors and actuators with Java to build powerful and scalable IoT systems.

9. **Performance Optimization**: Building performant applications is essential for scalability and user satisfaction. We cover **profiling tools**, **code optimization strategies**, and practical techniques to improve application performance.

10. **Emerging Trends**: Finally, we explore cutting-edge Java trends like **GraalVM**, **modularization**, and **Project Loom**, which are shaping the future of Java development.

Real-World Examples

A crucial aspect of learning any programming language is applying it to real-world problems. This book not only focuses on theory but also provides **hands-on examples** that simulate real-world applications:

- **Building a Java-based E-commerce System**: Develop a scalable and maintainable **e-commerce application** using **Java Spring Boot**, integrating it with **databases, RESTful APIs,** and handling **user authentication** and **authorization**.

- **IoT-based Home Automation**: Learn to use **Java** in **IoT systems** by creating a smart **home automation system** that controls devices like lights and sensors using **MQTT** and **Raspberry Pi**.

- **Real-Time Data Processing**: We'll guide you through the development of an **asynchronous real-time data stream processing system**, leveraging **Java Reactive Programming** to process and react to continuous data streams, such as stock prices or sensor readings.

- **Optimizing a Java Web Application for Performance**: Using **profiling tools** like **VisualVM** and **JProfiler**, we'll show you how to identify and address performance bottlenecks in a web application, leading to faster load times and improved resource utilization.

Why This Book Is for You

Whether you are an experienced Java developer or someone just starting out, this book is designed to enhance your Java skills and provide practical insights that will help you work on **complex projects**. By the end of this book, you will:

- Gain **in-depth knowledge** of core Java features and advanced programming techniques.
- Be proficient in **building cloud-based Java applications**, optimizing performance, and handling real-time data.
- Understand how to leverage **modern Java tools** for **microservices**, **big data**, and **IoT**.
- Be prepared for the **future of Java development** by learning about the latest trends and technologies such as **GraalVM** and **Project Loom**.

This book provides a structured approach to mastering Java for modern, complex projects, and is an invaluable resource for developers who want to stay ahead in the rapidly evolving software development landscape.

Conclusion

"Mastering Java for Complex Projects" is more than just a guide to Java; it's an in-depth exploration of the Java ecosystem and its role in building sophisticated, modern applications. As Java continues to evolve, mastering it will open doors to a wide array of exciting opportunities in various fields, from cloud computing and data science to Internet of Things and reactive programming.

With this book, you will not only learn Java but also gain the knowledge and confidence to take on complex development challenges and create applications that stand the test of time. Let's dive into the world of Java and unlock its full potential for building powerful, scalable, and resilient systems!

CHAPTER 1

INTRODUCTION TO ADVANCED JAVA PROGRAMMING

This chapter serves as an introduction to advanced Java programming, providing readers with the foundational understanding of Java's importance in the software development world. It sets the stage for the deeper dive into more complex topics covered in the subsequent chapters.

Overview of Java's Role in Modern Development

Java has been one of the most influential programming languages in the development of enterprise-level applications, web services, mobile apps, and more. Its portability, scalability, and security have made it a staple in the tech industry. Java is a versatile language that powers everything from large-scale corporate systems to Android apps and embedded devices.

- **Platform Independence**: The famous phrase "write once, run anywhere" is central to Java's philosophy. Java code is compiled into bytecode, which can be executed on any system with a Java Virtual Machine (JVM). This makes Java one of the most cross-platform friendly languages.

13

- **Enterprise Solutions**: Java is widely used in the creation of large-scale systems for banking, telecommunications, retail, and healthcare sectors. It provides a strong backbone for applications that require high reliability, security, and the ability to scale efficiently.

- **Android Development**: Java has played a major role in Android development, making it one of the dominant languages for building mobile applications. While Kotlin has gained popularity in recent years, Java remains an essential skill for Android developers.

- **Big Data and Cloud Services**: With the rise of big data technologies and cloud computing, Java has maintained its relevance by being integrated into popular big data platforms like Apache Hadoop and Spark. It also supports cloud services through frameworks like Spring Boot for building microservices.

Key Features and Advantages of Java

Java's popularity can be attributed to several of its key features that make it stand out among other programming languages. Some of the most important ones include:

- **Object-Oriented**: Java follows object-oriented principles, which promote code reusability, scalability, and maintainability. This is especially important in large

14

projects, where a modular and organized codebase is crucial.

- **Portability**: As mentioned, Java code runs on any platform that supports JVM. This platform independence allows developers to write code that works across different operating systems without modification.

- **Performance**: Java's performance is enhanced by Just-In-Time (JIT) compilation, which compiles bytecode into native machine code at runtime. This makes Java fast and efficient, though it may still not be as quick as languages like C++ in certain areas.

- **Security**: Java has built-in security features like the bytecode verifier, runtime security manager, and robust APIs that help prevent malicious activities. This makes Java particularly well-suited for building secure applications, such as those used in banking or enterprise environments.

- **Rich API**: Java comes with a vast set of libraries and frameworks that provide ready-to-use functions, allowing developers to focus on business logic instead of reinventing the wheel. These libraries span areas like networking, file I/O, databases, and graphical user interfaces (GUIs).

- **Concurrency**: Java provides built-in support for multi-threading, which is essential for building applications that need to handle multiple tasks concurrently. The ability to

15

write efficient multi-threaded applications is critical in high-performance systems like gaming engines or server-side applications.

- **Large Developer Community**: Java has a huge, active community of developers, which means an abundance of resources, libraries, tools, and frameworks. Java's community-driven approach ensures that the language keeps evolving and stays relevant in the rapidly changing tech world.

Setting Up a Java Development Environment

Before you can start building advanced Java applications, you need to set up a development environment. Here's a simple guide to getting started:

1. **Install the Java Development Kit (JDK)**:
   - The JDK includes everything you need to write, compile, and run Java applications, including the Java Runtime Environment (JRE) and Java compiler (javac).
   - You can download the latest version of JDK from the official Oracle website or use OpenJDK, which is an open-source version.

2. **Install an Integrated Development Environment (IDE)**:

- An IDE is essential for efficient Java development. It provides features like code completion, debugging, and project management. There are several popular IDEs for Java development:
  - **IntelliJ IDEA**: Known for its intelligent code suggestions, debugging tools, and integration with version control systems like Git.
  - **Eclipse**: A highly customizable and feature-rich IDE used by both beginner and expert developers.
  - **NetBeans**: A free and open-source IDE that offers a simple interface and great support for web applications and Java EE development.

3. **Set Up Version Control**:
   - Git is the most widely used version control system. Setting up a Git repository allows you to track changes to your code and collaborate with other developers.
   - Services like GitHub, GitLab, and Bitbucket offer cloud-hosted repositories, making it easier to manage your codebase and share your work.

4. **Verify Your Setup**:

- o After installation, open your terminal or command prompt and type `java -version` to check that Java is installed correctly. You should see the version number of the JDK you installed.
- o Additionally, try running `javac -version` to check the compiler installation.

Introduction to Java IDEs and Tools

In this section, we'll dive into the features of the most commonly used Java IDEs and tools that will help streamline development and improve productivity.

- **IntelliJ IDEA**:
  - o IntelliJ is known for its smart code completion, code analysis, and refactoring tools. It has excellent support for modern Java frameworks like Spring and Hibernate.
  - o It also integrates seamlessly with build tools like Maven and Gradle, making it easy to manage dependencies and handle project configurations.
  - o **Real-World Example**: Use IntelliJ to quickly set up and deploy a Spring Boot-based microservice application, utilizing its built-in Spring support for auto-completion and live templates.
- **Eclipse**:

- o Eclipse is widely regarded as a robust IDE for Java development. It has a large number of plugins that enhance its capabilities, from support for JavaFX to cloud development and database integration.
- o It includes built-in tools for debugging, profiling, and testing. Eclipse is highly extensible, allowing developers to install custom plugins based on project needs.
- o **Real-World Example**: Develop and debug a multi-threaded Java application that interacts with a MySQL database using Eclipse's debugging tools.
- **NetBeans**:
  - o NetBeans is an easy-to-use IDE, especially for beginners. It provides an integrated development environment for Java SE, Java EE, and web applications. It also has built-in support for various Java frameworks, making it a great choice for enterprise development.
  - o NetBeans offers features like GUI builders for designing desktop applications and integration with various version control systems.
  - o **Real-World Example**: Use NetBeans to quickly build a Java desktop application for personal

finance management, utilizing its drag-and-drop GUI builder for a smooth user experience.

- **Additional Tools**:
  - o **Maven**: A build automation tool that simplifies project dependency management, ensuring your Java projects always have the required libraries and frameworks.
  - o **Gradle**: Another build tool, commonly used in Android development, known for its flexibility and scalability.
  - o **JUnit and TestNG**: Frameworks for unit testing in Java, which help ensure code reliability and robustness.

This chapter lays the foundation for all future topics in your Java programming journey. By understanding the role of Java in modern development and setting up the right environment, you'll be ready to dive deeper into the complexities of advanced Java topics. In the next chapter, we'll revisit the basics and reinforce the concepts needed to tackle more complex challenges in Java programming.

CHAPTER 2

JAVA LANGUAGE BASICS REFRESHER

In this chapter, we will refresh some of the fundamental concepts in Java. While these concepts may be familiar to those with basic programming experience, they form the essential building blocks for more advanced topics. A solid understanding of Java's syntax, control flow, and object-oriented principles is crucial before diving into more complex applications.

Variables, Data Types, and Operators

Understanding how to declare and use variables, as well as knowing the various data types in Java, is fundamental to writing any Java application.

- **Variables**: Variables in Java store data and are associated with a specific data type. Each variable must be declared with a type before it can be used. The type dictates the kind of data the variable can store.
  - **Syntax**: `dataType variableName = value;`
  - Example:

```java
java

int age = 25;
String name = "John";
double price = 19.99;
```

- **Data Types**: Java is a statically typed language, meaning the type of a variable must be defined at the time of declaration. Java provides several built-in data types:
  - **Primitive Types**:
    - `byte`: 8-bit signed integer
    - `short`: 16-bit signed integer
    - `int`: 32-bit signed integer
    - `long`: 64-bit signed integer
    - `float`: 32-bit floating point
    - `double`: 64-bit floating point
    - `char`: 16-bit Unicode character
    - `boolean`: true or false
  - **Reference Types**:
    - Objects (e.g., instances of classes like `String`, `ArrayList`)
- **Operators**: Java supports a wide range of operators, including:
  - **Arithmetic Operators**: +, -, *, /, %
  - **Relational Operators**: ==, !=, >, <, >=, <=
  - **Logical Operators**: && (AND), || (OR), ! (NOT)

22

- o **Assignment Operators**: =, +=, -=, *=, /=
- o **Unary Operators**: ++ (increment), -- (decrement)
- o **Ternary Operator**: `condition ? trueExpression : falseExpression`

Control Flow: Loops and Conditional Statements

Control flow structures allow your program to make decisions and repeat certain actions. These are the basic building blocks for any program logic.

- **Conditional Statements**: Java provides several conditional statements to perform actions based on certain conditions.
  - o **if Statement**:

    ```java

    if (x > 10) {
        System.out.println("x is greater than 10");
    }
    ```

  - o **else if Statement**:

    ```java
    ```

```java
if (x > 10) {
    System.out.println("x is greater
than 10");
} else if (x < 10) {
    System.out.println("x   is   less
than 10");
} else {
    System.out.println("x   is   equal
to 10");
}
```

- o **switch Statement** (used when checking multiple conditions):

```java
java

switch (dayOfWeek) {
    case                    1:
System.out.println("Monday"); break;
    case                    2:
System.out.println("Tuesday");
break;
    default:
System.out.println("Invalid day");
}
```

- **Loops**: Loops are used to repeat actions a certain number of times or while a condition is true.

o **for Loop**: A `for` loop is generally used when the number of iterations is known in advance.

java

```java
for (int i = 0; i < 10; i++) {
    System.out.println(i);
}
```

o **while Loop**: A `while` loop is used when the number of iterations is not known and depends on a condition.

java

```java
int i = 0;
while (i < 10) {
    System.out.println(i);
    i++;
}
```

o **do-while Loop**: A `do-while` loop guarantees at least one iteration, even if the condition is false.

java

```java
int i = 0;
do {
    System.out.println(i);
```

```
        i++;
    } while (i < 10);
```

Functions, Methods, and Recursion

- **Functions and Methods**: In Java, functions are referred to as methods. Methods define the behavior of objects and can be invoked to perform actions.
    - **Defining a Method**: A method must have a return type, a name, and parameters (optional). The return type defines what kind of value the method will return (e.g., int, String, void).
        - **Syntax**:

        ```java

        returnType
        methodName(parameters) {
            // method body
        }
        ```

        - Example:

        ```java

        public    int    addNumbers(int
        num1, int num2) {
            return num1 + num2;
        ```

26

```
}
```

o **Method Overloading**: Java supports method overloading, where multiple methods can have the same name but different parameter lists.

java

```java
public int addNumbers(int num1, int num2) {
    return num1 + num2;
}

public double addNumbers(double num1, double num2) {
    return num1 + num2;
}
```

o **Method Return Types**: A method can return values of various types, such as int, boolean, or String. If a method doesn't return anything, it is declared with the void return type.

java

```java
public void displayMessage(String message) {
    System.out.println(message);
}
```

- **Recursion**: Recursion is a method calling itself to solve smaller instances of the same problem. While it can be powerful, it must have a termination condition to avoid infinite recursion.

  o Example of a recursive method to calculate the factorial of a number:

  java

  ```java
  public int factorial(int n) {
      if (n == 0) {
          return 1;
      } else {
          return n * factorial(n - 1);
      }
  }
  ```

  o **Real-World Example**: Recursion is often used in problems involving tree structures, like traversing a file directory or calculating the Fibonacci series.

Object-Oriented Programming Concepts (Classes, Objects, Inheritance)

Object-Oriented Programming (OOP) is one of the core paradigms of Java and allows developers to model real-world entities through classes and objects.

- **Classes and Objects**:
  - o **Class**: A class is a blueprint for creating objects. It defines fields (variables) and methods that determine the behavior of an object.
  - o **Object**: An object is an instance of a class. It is created using the `new` keyword.
    - **Example**:

```java

public class Car {
    String model;
    int year;

    public                    void
    displayDetails() {

    System.out.println("Model: " +
    model + ", Year: " + year);
        }
    }

    // Creating an object of the
    class
    Car myCar = new Car();
    myCar.model = "Toyota";
    myCar.year = 2020;
    myCar.displayDetails();
```

- **Inheritance**: Inheritance allows a class to inherit properties and behaviors from another class. The class that is inherited from is called the **superclass**, and the class that inherits is called the **subclass**.

  o **Syntax**:

  java

  ```java
  class Subclass extends Superclass {
      // additional fields and methods
  }
  ```

  o Example:

  java

  ```java
  class Animal {
      String name;

      public void speak() {
          System.out.println("Animal
  is making a sound");
      }
  }

  class Dog extends Animal {
      public void speak() {
          System.out.println("Dog
  barks");
  ```

```
        }
}

Dog myDog = new Dog();
myDog.name = "Buddy";
myDog.speak();  // Output: Dog barks
```

o **Polymorphism**: Java allows the same method to behave differently depending on the object that invokes it. This is called polymorphism.

```java

Animal myAnimal = new Animal();
myAnimal.speak();     // Animal is making a sound

Animal myDog = new Dog();
myDog.speak();  // Dog barks
```

- **Encapsulation and Abstraction**:
  - o **Encapsulation** is the practice of keeping fields within a class private and providing access to them via public methods (getters and setters).
  - o **Abstraction** involves hiding the complex implementation and showing only the necessary details to the user.

This chapter reinforces Java's core language constructs, which are essential for writing both simple and complex applications. A solid grasp of variables, control flow, methods, and object-oriented principles is crucial as we move on to more advanced concepts in later chapters.

CHAPTER 3

OBJECT-ORIENTED PROGRAMMING IN DEPTH

In this chapter, we will dive deeper into the principles of Object-Oriented Programming (OOP) and explore how they are implemented in Java. OOP is a powerful paradigm that allows developers to model real-world problems through classes and objects. We'll also look at some design patterns that can help make your code more flexible, maintainable, and reusable.

Encapsulation, Inheritance, and Polymorphism

These are the three core principles of Object-Oriented Programming. Understanding how to implement and use them effectively is crucial for developing scalable and maintainable applications in Java.

- **Encapsulation**: Encapsulation refers to the concept of bundling the data (fields) and methods that operate on the data into a single unit called a class. It also involves restricting access to certain components of an object to ensure that the object's data is protected from unintended interference and misuse.

- o **Access Modifiers**: The primary way to achieve encapsulation in Java is through access modifiers like `private`, `protected`, and `public`.

  - **Private**: The field or method is accessible only within the same class.
  - **Public**: The field or method is accessible from anywhere.
  - **Protected**: The field or method is accessible within the same package or subclasses.
  - **Default**: If no modifier is specified, the field or method is accessible within the same package.

- o **Example**:

```java
java


public class Car {
    // Private fields
    private String model;
    private int year;

    // Public getter method for model
    public String getModel() {
        return model;
    }

    // Public setter method for model
```

```
public    void    setModel(String
model) {
      this.model = model;
   }
}
```

In this example, the `model` field is private and cannot be accessed directly from outside the class. Instead, we use getter and setter methods to read and update the field.

- **Inheritance**: Inheritance allows one class (the subclass) to inherit fields and methods from another class (the superclass). This promotes code reusability and a hierarchical relationship between classes.

    o **Syntax**:

    java

    ```
    class Subclass extends Superclass {
        // Subclass-specific code
    }
    ```

    o **Example**:

    java

    ```
    class Animal {
        public void speak() {
    ```

35

```
        System.out.println("Animal
speaks");
    }
}

class Dog extends Animal {
    public void speak() {
        System.out.println("Dog
barks");
    }
}

Dog dog = new Dog();
dog.speak();  // Output: Dog barks
```

In this example, Dog inherits the speak method from Animal, but it overrides it to provide its specific implementation.

- **Polymorphism**: Polymorphism allows objects to be treated as instances of their parent class. It enables a single method to behave differently depending on the object calling it.
  - **Example**:

```
java

Animal animal = new Dog();
animal.speak();  // Output: Dog barks
```

In this case, even though `animal` is declared as an `Animal`, it refers to a `Dog` object, which overrides the `speak` method.

Abstraction and Interfaces in Java

- **Abstraction**: Abstraction involves hiding the complexity of an implementation and exposing only the necessary details to the user. This is achieved through abstract classes or interfaces.
  - **Abstract Classes**: An abstract class cannot be instantiated directly. It is used as a base class for other classes. Abstract methods (methods without a body) are defined in the abstract class and must be implemented by subclasses.
    - **Example**:

```java

abstract class Animal {
    abstract void speak();  //
Abstract method
}

class Dog extends Animal {
    @Override
    void speak() {
```

37

```
System.out.println("Dog
barks");
    }
}
```

- **Interfaces**: An interface is a contract that defines a set of abstract methods that the implementing class must provide. Java allows a class to implement multiple interfaces, which helps in creating flexible and extensible applications.
  - **Example**:

```java
interface Animal {
    void speak();  // Abstract method
in interface
}

class Dog implements Animal {
    @Override
    public void speak() {
        System.out.println("Dog
barks");
    }
}
```

- In this example, the `Dog` class implements the `Animal` interface and provides an implementation for the `speak` method.

Design Patterns: Singleton, Factory, and Observer Patterns

Design patterns provide general solutions to common problems in software design. By using design patterns, you can ensure that your code is more reusable, flexible, and maintainable.

- **Singleton Pattern**: The Singleton pattern ensures that a class has only one instance and provides a global point of access to that instance.
    - **Example**:

```java
public class Singleton {
    private static Singleton instance;

    private Singleton() { }

    public static Singleton getInstance() {
        if (instance == null) {
            instance = new Singleton();
```

```
        }
        return instance;
    }
}
```

- In this example, the `Singleton` class has a private constructor to prevent direct instantiation. The `getInstance()` method ensures that only one instance of the class exists.

- **Factory Pattern**: The Factory pattern provides an interface for creating objects but allows subclasses to alter the type of objects that will be created.

  o **Example**:

```java
interface Animal {
    void speak();
}

class Dog implements Animal {
    public void speak() {
        System.out.println("Dog barks");
    }
}

class Cat implements Animal {
    public void speak() {
```

```
        System.out.println("Cat
meows");
    }
}

class AnimalFactory {
    public     static     Animal
getAnimal(String type) {
        if (type.equals("dog")) {
            return new Dog();
        } else         if
(type.equals("cat")) {
            return new Cat();
        }
        return null;
    }
}
```

- In this example, the `AnimalFactory` class provides a method to create `Dog` or `Cat` objects based on the input.
- **Observer Pattern**: The Observer pattern is used when one object (the subject) changes state and all its dependents (observers) are notified automatically. It is commonly used in implementing event handling systems.
  - **Example**:

```
java

interface Observer {
```

```java
    void update(String message);
}

class ConcreteObserver implements
Observer {
    private String name;

    public ConcreteObserver(String
name) {
        this.name = name;
    }

    public void update(String
message) {
        System.out.println(name + "
received message: " + message);
    }
}

class Subject {
    private List<Observer> observers
= new ArrayList<>();

    public void addObserver(Observer
observer) {
        observers.add(observer);
    }
```

```
public                          void
removeObserver(Observer observer) {
        observers.remove(observer);
    }

    public                          void
notifyObservers(String message) {
        for  (Observer  observer  :
observers) {

observer.update(message);
        }
    }
}
```

- In this example, the `Subject` class maintains a list of observers and notifies them when an event occurs.

Real-World Example: Building a Simple CRUD Application

Now, let's put everything together by building a simple CRUD (Create, Read, Update, Delete) application in Java. We will use the concepts of encapsulation, inheritance, and polymorphism, as well as implement a simple factory pattern for managing different types of data storage.

- **Step 1: Define the Data Model**:

43

```java
java

class Product {
    private int id;
    private String name;
    private double price;

    public Product(int id, String name,
double price) {
        this.id = id;
        this.name = name;
        this.price = price;
    }

    public int getId() {
        return id;
    }

    public String getName() {
        return name;
    }

    public double getPrice() {
        return price;
    }

    @Override
    public String toString() {
```

```
        return "Product [id=" + id + ",
name=" + name + ", price=" + price + "]";
    }
}
```

- **Step 2: Create the CRUD Operations**:

```java
class ProductService {
    private Map<Integer, Product> products
= new HashMap<>();

    public void createProduct(int id,
String name, double price) {
        Product product = new Product(id,
name, price);
        products.put(id, product);
    }

    public Product readProduct(int id) {
        return products.get(id);
    }

    public void updateProduct(int id,
String name, double price) {
        Product product =
products.get(id);
        if (product != null) {
```

```java
        product   =   new   Product(id,
name, price);
            products.put(id, product);
        }
    }


    public void deleteProduct(int id) {
        products.remove(id);
    }
}
```

- **Step 3: Demonstrate CRUD Operations**:

```java
java

public class Main {
    public static void main(String[] args)
{
        ProductService   service   =   new
ProductService();
        service.createProduct(1, "Laptop",
1200.00);
        service.createProduct(2,
"Smartphone", 799.99);


System.out.println(service.readProduct(1)
);
        service.updateProduct(1,   "Laptop
Pro", 1500.00);
```

```
System.out.println(service.readProduct(1)
);

        service.deleteProduct(2);

System.out.println(service.readProduct(2)
);   // null
    }
}
```

This simple CRUD application demonstrates key object-oriented concepts such as encapsulation, object creation, and updates, and how to structure a Java application for real-world use cases.

This chapter has given you a solid foundation in Java's object-oriented features, which are essential for building robust and maintainable applications. In the next chapter, we will look at more advanced features and tools in Java.

CHAPTER 4

EXCEPTION HANDLING AND DEBUGGING

Exception handling is a crucial part of Java programming, ensuring that programs can handle unexpected situations or errors gracefully without crashing. Debugging, on the other hand, is the process of finding and fixing bugs (errors) in your code. In this chapter, we will explore how Java handles exceptions, how to create custom exceptions, and how to debug your code efficiently.

Java's Exception Hierarchy

Java has a well-defined exception hierarchy, which categorizes different types of errors that can occur during the execution of a program. Understanding this hierarchy will help you handle exceptions more effectively.

- **Throwable Class**:
  - o The root class for all errors and exceptions in Java is Throwable. It has two main subclasses:
    - **Error**: These are serious issues that a program cannot typically handle. Examples include OutOfMemoryError

and `StackOverflowError`. Errors are not meant to be caught by application code.

- **Exception**: These represent conditions that a program can handle. Most exceptions in Java are subclasses of the `Exception` class.

- **Checked Exceptions**:
  - These are exceptions that are checked at compile time. They must be either caught or declared in the method signature using the `throws` keyword.
  - Examples include `IOException`, `SQLException`, and `FileNotFoundException`.

- **Unchecked Exceptions**:
  - These exceptions do not need to be explicitly handled. They are subclasses of `RuntimeException`. These are typically caused by programming bugs, such as logical errors or incorrect use of the API.
  - Examples include `NullPointerException`, `ArrayIndexOutOfBoundsException`, and `ArithmeticException`.

- **Error vs. Exception**:
  - **Error**: Typically external to the application (e.g., hardware failure).

- o **Exception**: Conditions that a program can usually handle (e.g., file not found, invalid input).

Example of Exception Hierarchy:

java

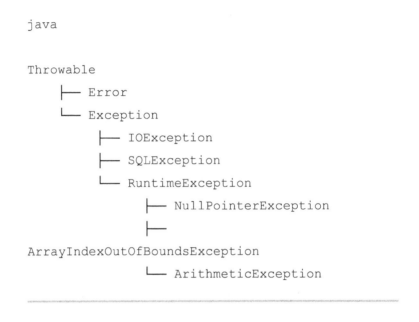

```
Throwable
    ├── Error
    └── Exception
            ├── IOException
            ├── SQLException
            └── RuntimeException
                    ├── NullPointerException
                    ├──
ArrayIndexOutOfBoundsException
                    └── ArithmeticException
```

Throwing, Catching, and Handling Exceptions

Handling exceptions allows your program to recover from errors without crashing. Java provides mechanisms for throwing, catching, and handling exceptions.

- **Throwing Exceptions**: To throw an exception, you can use the `throw` keyword. This can be done explicitly within your methods to signal an error or invalid condition.

50

o Example:

```
java
```

```java
public void divide(int a, int b) {
    if (b == 0) {
        throw                      new
ArithmeticException("Cannot    divide
by zero");
    }
    System.out.println(a / b);
}
```

- **Catching Exceptions**: Exceptions are caught using a
  try-catch block. Code that might throw an exception is
  enclosed in the try block, and the catch block handles
  the exception when it occurs.

  o Example:

```
java
```

```java
try {
    int result = divide(10, 0);
} catch (ArithmeticException e) {
    System.out.println("Error:   "  +
e.getMessage());
}
```

- **Finally Block**: The `finally` block is optional and is always executed whether or not an exception occurs. It is typically used to close resources such as files or database connections.

  o Example:

  ```java
  try {
      // Some code that might throw an
  exception
  } catch (Exception e) {
      // Handle exception
  } finally {
      System.out.println("This     will
  always run");
  }
  ```

- **Throws Keyword**: In Java, if a method can throw an exception, you must declare it using the `throws` keyword in the method signature. This informs the calling code that it needs to handle or propagate the exception.

  o Example:

  ```java
  public      void      readFile(String
  filename) throws IOException {
  ```

```
    FileReader    file    =    new
FileReader(filename);
    // Read the file
}
```

Custom Exception Classes

Sometimes, the built-in exceptions do not suit your application's needs. In these cases, you can create your own custom exception classes. Custom exceptions help make your code more readable and can convey specific error information related to your domain.

- **Creating a Custom Exception**: A custom exception class is typically a subclass of Exception (for checked exceptions) or RuntimeException (for unchecked exceptions).

  o Example:

  ```java
  public    class    InvalidAgeException
  extends Exception {
      public
  InvalidAgeException(String    message)
  {
          super(message);
      }
  }
  ```

53

- **Using the Custom Exception**: Once you've defined a custom exception, you can throw it in your code when a specific error condition occurs.
  o Example:

```java
public class Registration {
    public void registerUser(String
username,     int     age)     throws
InvalidAgeException {
        if (age < 18) {
            throw             new
InvalidAgeException("Age must be 18
or older");
        }
        // Proceed with registration
    }
}
```

- **Handling the Custom Exception**: You can catch and handle custom exceptions just like any other exception.
  o Example:

```java
public class Main {
    public static void main(String[]
args) {
```

```
        Registration  registration  =
new Registration();
        try {

registration.registerUser("JohnDoe"
, 16);
        } catch (InvalidAgeException
e) {

System.out.println("Registration
failed: " + e.getMessage());
        }
    }
}
```

Debugging Techniques and Tools

Debugging is an essential skill in software development, allowing you to find and fix issues in your code. Java provides various tools and techniques to assist with debugging.

- **Using Print Statements**: The simplest form of debugging involves adding print statements at various points in your code to monitor variable values and program flow.
  - o Example:

```java
```

```
System.out.println("Value of x:  " +
x);
```

- **Using a Debugger**: Modern IDEs such as IntelliJ IDEA, Eclipse, and NetBeans have built-in debuggers that allow you to step through your code, examine variables, and control execution flow.

  o **Breakpoints**: You can set breakpoints in your code to pause execution at specific lines, allowing you to inspect the state of your program.

  o **Step Through Code**: Step through your program one line at a time to understand how it's executing and where things might go wrong.

  o **Watch Expressions**: Watches allow you to monitor specific variables and expressions while debugging, providing real-time information about their values.

Example using IntelliJ IDEA:

4.   Set a breakpoint by clicking in the left margin of the editor.

5.   Start debugging by clicking the debug button.

6.   Use "Step Over" to move through the code, "Step Into" to go inside methods, and "Step Out" to exit methods.

- **Exception Stack Trace**: When an exception occurs, Java provides a stack trace that shows the sequence of method calls leading to the error. This can help identify the root cause of the problem.
  - Example:

```java

try {
    // Code that throws an exception
} catch (Exception e) {
    e.printStackTrace();
}
```

- The stack trace output will show where the exception occurred and the path the program took to reach that point.
- **Profiling Tools**: Profiling tools help you analyze your program's performance, including memory usage, CPU usage, and thread activity. Java provides tools like **VisualVM** and **JProfiler** for profiling your application and identifying performance bottlenecks.
- **Logging**: Instead of using print statements, it is often better to use a logging framework (such as **Log4j** or **SLF4J**) for more sophisticated logging. These tools allow you to log messages at different levels (e.g., INFO, DEBUG, ERROR), and you can configure them to write logs to files, making it easier to trace issues in production environments.

- o **Example with Log4j**:

```java
import org.apache.log4j.Logger;

public class Main {
    final static Logger logger =
Logger.getLogger(Main.class);

    public static void main(String[]
args) {
        logger.info("Application
started");
        try {
            // Some code
        } catch (Exception e) {
            logger.error("An    error
occurred: " + e.getMessage());
        }
    }
}
```

By understanding how Java handles exceptions, creating custom exceptions when necessary, and utilizing effective debugging tools, you can significantly improve the quality and reliability of your applications. In the next chapter, we will explore how to work with collections and data structures in Java.

CHAPTER 5

WORKING WITH COLLECTIONS IN JAVA

In this chapter, we will explore the powerful Java Collections Framework, which provides a set of classes and interfaces to handle groups of objects. Understanding how to use collections effectively is key to developing efficient Java applications, as they allow you to store, retrieve, and manipulate data in a structured way. We will cover different types of collections, advanced operations, and provide a real-world example of implementing an inventory management system.

Introduction to Collections Framework

The Java Collections Framework is a unified architecture for representing and manipulating collections of objects. It provides interfaces and classes that allow you to work with data in various ways, from simple lists to complex data structures.

The key components of the Collections Framework are:

- **Interfaces**: These define common behaviors that all collections implement. The most important interfaces are `Collection`, `List`, `Set`, `Map`, and `Queue`.

- **Implementations**: These are concrete classes that provide specific implementations of the interfaces. For example, `ArrayList`, `HashSet`, and `HashMap`.

- **Algorithms**: These are utility methods that operate on collections, such as sorting, reversing, and searching.

- **Comparators and Iterators**: These help in custom sorting and iteration through collections.

Lists, Sets, Maps, and Queues

Java provides several types of collections for different use cases. Let's dive into some of the most commonly used types:

- **List**:
  - A `List` is an ordered collection that allows duplicates. It maintains the order of insertion and allows elements to be accessed by their index.
  - Common implementations: `ArrayList`, `LinkedList`, `Vector`.
  - **Example**:

    ```java
    java
    ```

```
List<String>     list     =     new
ArrayList<>();
list.add("Apple");
list.add("Banana");
list.add("Apple");
System.out.println(list);          //
Output: [Apple, Banana, Apple]
```

- **Set**:
  - o A `Set` is an unordered collection that does not allow duplicates. It is useful when you need to ensure that no element is repeated.
  - o Common implementations: `HashSet`, `LinkedHashSet`, `TreeSet`.
  - o **Example**:

    ```java
    Set<String> set = new HashSet<>();
    set.add("Apple");
    set.add("Banana");
    set.add("Apple");  // Duplicate will
    not be added
    System.out.println(set);  // Output:
    [Apple, Banana]
    ```

- **Map**:
  - o A `Map` is a collection of key-value pairs, where each key is associated with exactly one value. It

61

does not allow duplicate keys but allows duplicate values.

o Common implementations: HashMap, TreeMap, LinkedHashMap.

o **Example**:

java

```
Map<Integer,  String>  map  =  new
HashMap<>();
map.put(1, "Apple");
map.put(2, "Banana");
map.put(1, "Orange");  // Overwrites
previous value for key 1
System.out.println(map);  // Output:
{1=Orange, 2=Banana}
```

- **Queue**:
  - o A Queue is a collection used to hold elements for processing. It follows the "first in, first out" (FIFO) principle.
  - o Common implementations: LinkedList, PriorityQueue.
  - o **Example**:

    java

```
Queue<String>      queue   =   new
LinkedList<>();
queue.add("Apple");
queue.add("Banana");
System.out.println(queue.poll());
// Output: Apple
System.out.println(queue);        //
Output: [Banana]
```

Advanced Operations on Collections

Once you have a solid understanding of the basic collections, it's time to explore some advanced operations that allow you to manipulate data efficiently.

- **Sorting**: Collections can be sorted using the `Collections.sort()` method or by using custom comparators.

  o **Example**:

  java

```
List<String>      list     =     new
ArrayList<>(Arrays.asList("Banana",
"Apple", "Mango"));
Collections.sort(list);
System.out.println(list);         //
Output: [Apple, Banana, Mango]
```

63

- **Custom Comparator**:

java

```
List<Integer> numbers = new
ArrayList<>(Arrays.asList(5,
2, 8, 1));
Collections.sort(numbers, (a,
b) -> b - a); // Sorting in
descending order
System.out.println(numbers);
// Output: [8, 5, 2, 1]
```

- **Searching**: You can search for elements in collections using methods like contains(), indexOf(), or binarySearch() (for sorted collections).
  - **Example**:

java

```
List<String> list = new
ArrayList<>(Arrays.asList("Apple",
"Banana", "Cherry"));
System.out.println(list.contains("B
anana")); // Output: true
System.out.println(list.indexOf("Ch
erry")); // Output: 2
```

- **Removing Elements**: Collections allow you to remove elements using `remove()`, `removeAll()`, or `clear()`.
    o **Example**:

    ```java
    List<String> list = new
    ArrayList<>(Arrays.asList("Apple",
    "Banana", "Apple"));
    list.remove("Apple");
    System.out.println(list);        //
    Output: [Banana, Apple]
    ```

- **Iteration**: Java provides several ways to iterate over collections:
    o **Enhanced for-loop**:

    ```java
    List<String> list =
    Arrays.asList("Apple", "Banana",
    "Cherry");
    for (String fruit : list) {
        System.out.println(fruit);
    }
    ```

    o **Iterator**:

    ```java
    ```

```
Iterator<String>        iterator        =
list.iterator();
while (iterator.hasNext()) {

System.out.println(iterator.next())
;
}
```

- **Concurrency in Collections**: Some collections, like `OnWriteArrayList` and `ConcurrentHashMap`, are designed for safe usage in multi-threaded environments.

Real-World Example: Implementing a Simple Inventory Management System

Let's put all this knowledge into practice by building a simple inventory management system. The system will allow us to add products to the inventory, update product details, and view the current inventory.

- **Step 1: Define the Product Class**: This class will represent each product in the inventory with an ID, name, and quantity.

```java
class Product {
    private int id;
```

```java
    private String name;
    private int quantity;

    public Product(int id, String name, int
quantity) {
        this.id = id;
        this.name = name;
        this.quantity = quantity;
    }

    public int getId() {
        return id;
    }

    public String getName() {
        return name;
    }

    public int getQuantity() {
        return quantity;
    }

    public void setQuantity(int  quantity)
{
        this.quantity = quantity;
    }

    @Override
    public String toString() {
```

```
        return "Product [ID=" + id + ",
Name=" + name + ", Quantity=" + quantity +
"]";
    }
}
```

- **Step 2: Create the Inventory Management System**: This class will manage a collection of products (using a Map), and provide methods to add, update, and display the inventory.

java

```
import java.util.HashMap;
import java.util.Map;

class InventorySystem {
    private Map<Integer, Product>
inventory = new HashMap<>();

    public void addProduct(int id, String
name, int quantity) {
        Product product = new Product(id,
name, quantity);
        inventory.put(id, product);
    }

    public void updateProductQuantity(int
id, int quantity) {
```

```
        Product            product          =
inventory.get(id);
        if (product != null) {

product.setQuantity(quantity);
        }
    }


    public void displayInventory() {
        for      (Product      product      :
inventory.values()) {
            System.out.println(product);
        }
    }
}
```

- **Step 3: Demonstrating the Inventory Management**:
  Here's how you can interact with the inventory system.

```java
public class Main {
    public static void main(String[] args)
{
        InventorySystem   system   =   new
InventorySystem();

        // Adding products to the inventory
        system.addProduct(1,     "Laptop",
10);
```

```
        system.addProduct(2, "Smartphone",
25);

        // Displaying inventory
        system.displayInventory();

        // Updating product quantity
        system.updateProductQuantity(1,
15);

        // Displaying updated inventory
        system.displayInventory();
    }
}
```

- **Output**:

```
mathematica

Product [ID=1, Name=Laptop, Quantity=10]
Product        [ID=2,        Name=Smartphone,
Quantity=25]
Product [ID=1, Name=Laptop, Quantity=15]
Product        [ID=2,        Name=Smartphone,
Quantity=25]
```

This chapter provided an overview of the Java Collections Framework and demonstrated how to work with various collection types like lists, sets, maps, and queues. You also learned about advanced operations and applied your knowledge to build a simple inventory management system. In the next chapter, we will dive into more advanced topics such as concurrency and multithreading.

CHAPTER 6

CONCURRENCY AND MULTITHREADING

Concurrency and multithreading are fundamental concepts for building high-performance, responsive applications in Java. This chapter will explore the essentials of threads in Java, how to handle synchronization and ensure thread safety, and how to use the Executor Service framework to manage threads efficiently. Finally, we will build a real-world example: a threaded file download manager.

Understanding Threads in Java

A **thread** is the smallest unit of execution within a program. Java provides built-in support for multithreading, which allows you to run multiple threads simultaneously. This is particularly useful for tasks that can be parallelized or when you want to perform long-running tasks (like file downloads or computations) without freezing the user interface.

- **Thread Basics**: In Java, a thread can be created in two ways:

1. **By extending the `Thread` class**: You can create a custom thread by extending the `Thread` class and overriding its `run()` method.

   - **Example**:

```java
class MyThread extends Thread
{
    @Override
    public void run() {

System.out.println("This    is
running    in    a    separate
thread.");
    }
}

public class Main {
    public    static    void
main(String[] args) {
        MyThread thread = new
MyThread();
        thread.start();    //
Starting the thread
    }
}
```

73

2. **By implementing the `Runnable` interface**: Alternatively, you can implement the Runnable interface and pass it to a Thread object.

- **Example**:

```java
class MyRunnable implements Runnable {
    @Override
    public void run() {

System.out.println("This is running in a separate thread.");
    }
}

public class Main {
    public static void main(String[] args) {
        MyRunnable myRunnable = new MyRunnable();
        Thread thread = new Thread(myRunnable);
        thread.start();    // Starting the thread
    }
}
```

74

- **Thread Lifecycle**: A thread goes through various states:
  1. **New**: A thread is created but not yet started.
  2. **Runnable**: The thread is ready to run but may not be running yet due to scheduling.
  3. **Blocked/Waiting**: The thread is waiting for resources or another thread.
  4. **Terminated**: The thread has finished execution.

Synchronization and Thread Safety

When multiple threads access shared resources (e.g., variables, data structures), synchronization is required to ensure data consistency and prevent race conditions. A **race condition** occurs when two or more threads attempt to modify shared data simultaneously, leading to unpredictable results.

- **Synchronization**: Java provides the `synchronized` keyword to prevent multiple threads from accessing a shared resource concurrently.
  - **Example**:

```java

class Counter {
    private int count = 0;
```

```
public      synchronized      void
increment() {
    count++;
}

public int getCount() {
    return count;
}
}
```

- In this example, the `increment()` method is synchronized, which ensures that only one thread can access it at a time.

- **Thread Safety**: In addition to using synchronization, you can make use of **thread-safe collections** like `ConcurrentHashMap` and **atomic variables** from the `java.util.concurrent.atomic` package to avoid synchronization issues.

  o **Example with `AtomicInteger`:**

```java
import
java.util.concurrent.atomic.AtomicI
nteger;

class Counter {
    private AtomicInteger count =
new AtomicInteger(0);
```

76

```
public void increment() {
    count.incrementAndGet();   //
Atomically increments the value
    }

public int getCount() {
    return count.get();
    }
}
```

The Executor Service Framework

Managing threads manually using `Thread` or `Runnable` can be cumbersome, especially when dealing with a large number of threads. The **Executor Service** framework provides a higher-level replacement for managing threads. It abstracts the thread creation and management process and provides a pool of threads that can be reused for different tasks.

- **Executor Service Basics**: The `ExecutorService` interface provides methods for managing and controlling a pool of threads. The most common implementation is `ThreadPoolExecutor`, which allows you to create a pool of worker threads.
  - **Example**:

    java

```
import
java.util.concurrent.ExecutorServic
e;
import
java.util.concurrent.Executors;

public class Main {
    public static void main(String[]
args) {
        ExecutorService
executorService                 =
Executors.newFixedThreadPool(3);  //
Pool of 3 threads

        for (int i = 0; i < 5; i++)
{

executorService.submit(() -> {

System.out.println(Thread.currentTh
read().getName() + " is executing a
task");
            });
        }

        executorService.shutdown();
// Shuts down the executor service
    }
```

```
}
```

- **Common Executors**: Java provides several factory methods in the Executors class to create different types of thread pools:

  o newFixedThreadPool(int nThreads): Creates a thread pool with a fixed number of threads.

  o newCachedThreadPool(): Creates a thread pool that can dynamically create new threads as needed.

  o newSingleThreadExecutor(): Creates a thread pool with a single worker thread.

Real-World Example: Building a Threaded File Download Manager

Now, let's put these concepts into practice by building a simple threaded file download manager. The manager will download multiple files simultaneously using a thread pool.

- **Step 1: Define the File Download Task**: We will create a DownloadTask class that implements the Runnable interface. Each task will simulate downloading a file by sleeping for a few seconds.

```java
```

```java
class DownloadTask implements Runnable {
    private String fileName;

    public DownloadTask(String fileName) {
        this.fileName = fileName;
    }

    @Override
    public void run() {
        try {
            System.out.println("Starting
download for: " + fileName);
            Thread.sleep(3000);           //
Simulate download time
            System.out.println("Download
complete for: " + fileName);
        } catch (InterruptedException e) {

Thread.currentThread().interrupt();
        }
    }
}
```

- **Step 2: Create the Download Manager**: The DownloadManager will use an ExecutorService to manage a pool of threads that will download multiple files concurrently.

```
java
```

```java
import
java.util.concurrent.ExecutorService;
import java.util.concurrent.Executors;

class DownloadManager {
    private            ExecutorService
executorService;

    public DownloadManager(int numThreads)
{
        executorService                =
Executors.newFixedThreadPool(numThreads);
// Create thread pool
    }

    public  void  downloadFiles(String[]
fileNames) {
        for (String fileName : fileNames)
{
            executorService.submit(new
DownloadTask(fileName));      //  Submit
download task
        }
    }

    public void shutdown() {
        executorService.shutdown();     //
Shutdown the thread pool
```

81

}

}

- **Step 3: Demonstrate the File Download Manager**: Here's the main class that demonstrates downloading multiple files using the DownloadManager.

java

```
public class Main {
    public static void main(String[] args)
{
        DownloadManager downloadManager =
new DownloadManager(3);    // Pool of 3
threads

        String[] fileNames = {"file1.txt",
"file2.jpg",   "file3.pdf",   "file4.zip",
"file5.mp4"};

downloadManager.downloadFiles(fileNames);

        downloadManager.shutdown();       //
Shutdown the executor service
    }
}
```

- **Output**:

yaml

```
Starting download for: file1.txt
Starting download for: file2.jpg
Starting download for: file3.pdf
Download complete for: file1.txt
Starting download for: file4.zip
Download complete for: file2.jpg
Download complete for: file3.pdf
Download complete for: file4.zip
Download complete for: file5.mp4
```

In this example, the `DownloadManager` class handles the concurrent downloading of multiple files using a thread pool. Each download task is executed in a separate thread, allowing them to run concurrently, which improves performance and responsiveness.

This chapter covered the key concepts of concurrency and multithreading in Java, including thread creation, synchronization, thread safety, and using the Executor Service framework. We also built a real-world example of a threaded file download manager to illustrate how these concepts come together in practice. In the next chapter, we will explore how to work with Java I/O for file handling and data processing.

83

CHAPTER 7

JAVA STREAMS AND LAMBDA EXPRESSIONS

In this chapter, we will explore functional programming concepts in Java, focusing on **lambda expressions** and **streams**. These features, introduced in Java 8, allow for more concise, readable, and efficient code when dealing with collections and other data structures. By leveraging **functional interfaces** and the **Streams API**, you can significantly simplify tasks such as data filtering, transformation, and aggregation.

Introduction to Functional Programming in Java

Functional programming is a programming paradigm where functions are treated as first-class citizens. In Java, functional programming was introduced in Java 8, enabling developers to write cleaner and more maintainable code. With the introduction of **lambda expressions**, **streams**, and **functional interfaces**, Java now supports a functional style of programming in addition to its object-oriented nature.

- **Functional Programming Concepts:**

○ **First-Class Functions**: Functions can be passed as arguments, returned as values, and assigned to variables.

○ **Immutability**: Data is not modified in place; instead, new data is returned when changes are needed.

○ **Higher-Order Functions**: Functions that take other functions as arguments or return functions as results.

○ **Pure Functions**: Functions that do not have side effects and return the same result for the same input.

Java's support for functional programming enables you to write more declarative code, focusing on **what** needs to be done rather than **how** it is done.

Using Lambda Expressions and Streams

• **Lambda Expressions**: A **lambda expression** in Java is a shorthand for writing anonymous methods (implementations of functional interfaces). It allows you to write compact and concise code for methods that are often used as arguments to higher-order functions, such as those found in streams.

○ **Syntax of Lambda Expressions**:

85

```java
```

```java
(parameters) -> expression
```

- **Example**:

```java
```

```java
// A simple lambda expression
to print a message
Runnable printMessage = () ->
System.out.println("Hello,
World!");
printMessage.run();          //
Output: Hello, World!
```

- **Lambda Expression with Parameters**:

```java
```

```java
(int a, int b) -> a + b  //
Lambda that adds two numbers
```

o **Lambda with Functional Interface**: Java 8 introduced **functional interfaces**, which are interfaces that have exactly one abstract method. Lambdas are used to provide the implementation for this single method.

- **Example**:

```java
interface Calculator {
    int calculate(int a, int b);
}

public class Main {
    public static void main(String[] args) {
        Calculator add = (a, b) -> a + b;

        System.out.println("Sum: " + add.calculate(5, 3)); // Output: Sum: 8
    }
}
```

- **Streams**: **Streams** represent a sequence of elements and support operations to process them. A stream does not modify the underlying data structure; it provides a way to manipulate data in a functional style (using operations like map, filter, reduce).
  - **Creating a Stream**: You can create a stream from a collection, array, or generator function.

```java
```

```
List<Integer>        numbers    =
Arrays.asList(1, 2, 3, 4, 5);
Stream<Integer>    numberStream    =
numbers.stream();
```

o **Stream Operations**:

- **Intermediate Operations**: These operations return a new stream and are lazy (they are not executed until a terminal operation is invoked).

  - **map()**: Transforms each element of the stream.

    ```java
    numbers.stream().map(n -
    >            n            *
    2).forEach(System.out::
    println);
    // Output: 2, 4, 6, 8, 10
    ```

  - **filter()**: Filters elements based on a condition.

    ```java
    numbers.stream().filter
    (n    ->    n    %    2    ==
    ```

```
0).forEach(System.out::
println);
// Output: 2, 4
```

- **Terminal Operations**: These operations trigger the processing of the stream and produce a result or a side effect.

    - **collect()**: Collects the elements of the stream into a collection.

    ```java
    List<Integer>
    evenNumbers          =
    numbers.stream()

    .filter(n -> n % 2 == 0)

    .collect(Collectors.toL
    ist());
    // evenNumbers: [2, 4]
    ```

    - **forEach()**: Iterates over the elements of the stream.

    ```java
    numbers.stream().forEac
    h(System.out::println);
    ```

89

- **reduce()**: Reduces the elements of the stream to a single value.

```java
int                sum              =
numbers.stream().reduce
(0, (a, b) -> a + b);
System.out.println("Sum
: " + sum);    // Output:
Sum: 15
```

The Power of Functional Interfaces

Java 8 introduced **functional interfaces**, which are interfaces with exactly one abstract method. These interfaces can be implemented using lambda expressions or method references.

- **Common Functional Interfaces**: Java provides several common functional interfaces in the java.util.function package:
  - **Predicate**: Represents a condition (boolean-valued function).

```java
Predicate<Integer> isEven = n -> n %
2 == 0;
```

```
System.out.println(isEven.test(4));
// Output: true
```

o **Function**: Represents a function that takes one argument and returns a result.

```java

Function<Integer, Integer> square =
n -> n * n;
System.out.println(square.apply(5))
;   // Output: 25
```

o **Consumer**: Represents an operation that accepts one input argument and returns no result.

```java

Consumer<String>    printMessage    =
message                          ->
System.out.println(message);
printMessage.accept("Hello,
World!");   // Output: Hello, World!
```

o **Supplier**: Represents a function that provides a result with no input.

```java

```

91

```
Supplier<Double> randomValue = () ->
Math.random();
System.out.println(randomValue.get(
));  // Output: Random value between
0.0 and 1.0
```

Real-World Example: Data Filtering and Transformation in a Business Application

Now, let's apply these concepts to a real-world example where we filter and transform data in a business application, such as a customer management system.

- **Step 1: Define a Customer Class**: The Customer class represents a customer in the system with an ID, name, and age.

java

```
class Customer {
    private int id;
    private String name;
    private int age;

    public Customer(int id, String name,
int age) {
        this.id = id;
        this.name = name;
```

```java
        this.age = age;
    }

    public int getId() {
        return id;
    }

    public String getName() {
        return name;
    }

    public int getAge() {
        return age;
    }

    @Override
    public String toString() {
        return "Customer{id=" + id + ",
name='" + name + "', age=" + age + "}";
    }
}
```

- **Step 2: Create a List of Customers**: We'll create a list of customers for our application.

```java
List<Customer> customers = Arrays.asList(
        new Customer(1, "Alice", 25),
        new Customer(2, "Bob", 30),
```

```
                    new Customer(3, "Charlie", 35),
                    new Customer(4, "Diana", 40),
                    new Customer(5, "Eve", 45)
);
```

- **Step 3: Filtering and Transformation with Streams**: Now, let's filter the customers based on age and transform their data.

  o **Filter**: Select customers who are older than 30.

  o **Map**: Transform the list to include only their names.

java

```java
List<String>        customerNames        =
customers.stream()
        .filter(customer                  ->
customer.getAge()   >   30)    //   Filter
customers by age
        .map(Customer::getName)           //
Extract the names of the filtered customers
        .collect(Collectors.toList());  //
Collect the results into a list

customerNames.forEach(System.out::println
);  // Output: Charlie, Diana, Eve
```

94

- **Step 4: Calculating Average Age**: We can also calculate the average age of customers using the `reduce()` method.

```java
double averageAge = customers.stream()
        .mapToInt(Customer::getAge)
        .average()
        .orElse(0.0);
System.out.println("Average    Age:    "    +
averageAge);  // Output: Average Age: 35.0
```

This chapter introduced **lambda expressions** and **streams**, showing how these powerful features of Java enable functional programming techniques. We also explored how **functional interfaces** allow for more flexible and concise code. Finally, we applied these concepts in a real-world scenario to filter and transform data in a business application, demonstrating how these features can simplify and optimize your Java code. In the next chapter, we will explore how to handle Java I/O operations and work with files and data streams.

CHAPTER 8

JAVA MEMORY MANAGEMENT AND GARBAGE COLLECTION

Memory management is an essential aspect of programming in Java, ensuring that your application runs efficiently and prevents memory-related issues, such as memory leaks. In this chapter, we will explore how Java manages memory, understand the Java Virtual Machine (JVM) architecture, and discuss the garbage collection process. Additionally, we will look at strategies to optimize memory usage and prevent memory leaks in large-scale applications.

Understanding Java Memory Model

The **Java Memory Model** (JMM) defines how Java programs interact with memory, specifying how variables are read from and written to the memory, and how threads access shared memory in a multithreaded environment.

- **Heap Memory**: The heap is where all objects (instances of classes) are stored. It is the primary area of memory that the JVM uses for dynamic memory allocation. The size of the heap is typically adjustable and can be modified using JVM options.

- o **Young Generation**: The part of the heap where new objects are allocated. It is further divided into:

  - **Eden Space**: Where new objects are created.

  - **Survivor Space**: Where objects that survive the young generation collection are moved.

- o **Old Generation**: The part of the heap where long-lived objects (those that survive several garbage collection cycles) are stored.

- **Stack Memory**: The stack stores method frames (local variables, method calls, etc.). Each thread has its own stack, and it is much smaller in size compared to the heap. The stack operates on a Last In, First Out (LIFO) basis, meaning that local variables and method calls are removed when the method execution completes.

- **Method Area**: The method area holds class-level data, such as the runtime constant pool, method and field data, and the code for methods and constructors.

- **Garbage Collection**: Java's memory management is largely automated through garbage collection, which automatically reclaims memory by removing unused objects.

JVM Architecture and Garbage Collection

The **Java Virtual Machine (JVM)** is responsible for executing Java bytecode and managing memory. It consists of several components, each serving a specific purpose in running Java applications.

- **JVM Components**:
    1. **Classloader**: Loads class files into memory.
    2. **Execution Engine**: Executes the bytecode instructions, either through interpretation or just-in-time (JIT) compilation.
    3. **Garbage Collector**: Reclaims memory used by objects that are no longer referenced, freeing up space in the heap.
    4. **Runtime Data Areas**: Memory regions where data is stored (heap, stack, method area, etc.).
- **Garbage Collection Process**: Garbage collection in Java is automatic, meaning the JVM identifies and reclaims memory used by unreachable objects (those no longer referenced by any active part of the program).

There are several types of garbage collection algorithms, including:

1. **Mark and Sweep**: The garbage collector marks all the objects that are reachable and then sweeps through the heap to delete objects that are not marked.

2. **Generational Garbage Collection**: Java's default garbage collector (the **Garbage-First** collector) divides the heap into the Young and Old generations. Objects are first allocated in the Young Generation, and after surviving several garbage collection cycles, they are promoted to the Old Generation.

3. **Stop-the-World Events**: During garbage collection, the JVM might pause application execution to perform memory cleanup. These pauses are known as "Stop-the-World" events, and while generally short, they can sometimes impact application performance.

- **Types of Garbage Collectors**: Java offers several garbage collectors optimized for different use cases:

  1. **Serial Garbage Collector**: Designed for small applications with a single thread.

  2. **Parallel Garbage Collector**: Uses multiple threads for garbage collection, providing better performance in multi-core systems.

3. **G1 Garbage Collector**: Balances throughput and pause times, commonly used for large-scale applications.

4. **Z Garbage Collector (ZGC)**: A low-latency collector designed for large heaps and multi-core systems.

Memory Leaks and Optimization Strategies

Despite Java's automated garbage collection, memory leaks can still occur if objects are inadvertently retained in memory. A **memory leak** happens when an application unintentionally retains references to objects that are no longer needed, preventing the garbage collector from reclaiming their memory.

- **Common Causes of Memory Leaks**:
    1. **Unclosed Resources**: Failing to close resources like database connections, file streams, or sockets can cause memory leaks.
    2. **Static References**: Objects stored in static variables are retained for the lifetime of the application, even if they are no longer needed.
    3. **Unintended Object Retention**: Storing objects in long-lived data structures (like caches or lists) and not removing them after they are no longer needed can lead to memory leaks.

100

4. **Listeners and Callbacks**: Registering listeners or callbacks without properly deregistering them can result in memory being retained unintentionally.

- **Strategies to Prevent Memory Leaks**:

1. **Close Resources**: Always close resources like file readers, database connections, and sockets using `finally` blocks or the try-with-resources statement.

java

```
try (BufferedReader reader = new
BufferedReader(new
FileReader("file.txt"))) {
    // Read file
} catch (IOException e) {
    // Handle exception
}
// Resources are automatically
closed
```

2. **Weak References**: Use `WeakReference` for objects that should be garbage collected when there are no strong references to them. This is useful for caches or listeners.

java

```
WeakReference<MyObject>   weakRef   =
new WeakReference<>(new MyObject());
```

3. **Avoid Unnecessary Static References**: Be mindful of storing large objects in static fields, as they will persist for the entire duration of the application.

4. **Use Profiling Tools**: Use memory profilers such as **VisualVM** or **Eclipse Memory Analyzer** (MAT) to detect memory leaks by analyzing heap dumps and identifying objects that are consuming too much memory.

Real-World Example: Analyzing Performance and Memory Usage in a Large-Scale Application

Let's consider a scenario where you are developing a large-scale business application. In such applications, it is critical to ensure memory efficiency to prevent performance degradation, especially when dealing with large datasets or long-running processes.

- **Step 1: Identifying Memory Usage**: In a large-scale system, memory usage can increase due to the accumulation of unnecessary objects in memory. By using a **memory profiler**, you can analyze memory usage and track object allocation.

- o **Using VisualVM**:
    1. **Heap Dump Analysis**: Take a heap dump during the application's execution to analyze which objects are consuming memory.
    2. **Class Histograms**: View the distribution of class instances and identify if any class is unexpectedly using a large amount of memory.
    3. **Garbage Collection Logs**: Enable garbage collection logging to understand how often garbage collection occurs and how much memory is being freed.
- **Step 2: Optimizing Memory Usage**:
    - o **Reduce Object Retention**: For example, if your application is processing a large number of customer records, ensure that customer objects are discarded or marked for garbage collection once they are no longer needed. You can store customer data temporarily in a `WeakHashMap` for caching, allowing them to be collected when the memory is needed.

- o **Lazy Loading**: Implement lazy loading for large datasets or resources. Load data only when required, rather than all at once.
- **Step 3: Performance Tuning**: After identifying the areas with high memory consumption, consider tuning the JVM settings:

  1. **Adjust Heap Size**: Increase the maximum heap size if your application requires more memory, or decrease it to limit memory usage in constrained environments.

```bash
java -Xmx4g -Xms2g -jar MyApp.jar  #
Set max heap to 4GB and initial heap
to 2GB
```

2. **Use G1 Garbage Collector**: If your application is large-scale, use the **G1 Garbage Collector** to manage memory more efficiently and reduce pause times.

  3. **Tuning Garbage Collection**: Enable garbage collection logging and adjust the GC settings for improved performance.

- **Step 4: Profiling and Monitoring**:
  - o Use tools like **JMX** (Java Management Extensions) to monitor memory usage and garbage collection in real-time. This can be

104

integrated into your production environment to track the health of the application and ensure that memory usage is kept under control.

This chapter covered essential concepts of **Java memory management**, including the JVM architecture, the process of garbage collection, memory leaks, and optimization strategies. Understanding how to manage memory and perform garbage collection effectively is vital for developing scalable and high-performance applications. By leveraging tools like **VisualVM** and adjusting JVM parameters, you can ensure that your application runs efficiently and remains responsive. In the next chapter, we will explore Java I/O operations for reading and writing files and data streams.

CHAPTER 9

BUILDING ROBUST APPLICATIONS WITH DESIGN PATTERNS

Design patterns are reusable solutions to common software design problems. They help developers write clean, efficient, and maintainable code. In this chapter, we will explore some common design patterns and how to implement them in Java. We will also see how refactoring an existing application using design patterns can improve its structure and flexibility.

Introduction to Common Design Patterns

Design patterns are categorized into three main groups:

- **Creational Patterns**: These patterns deal with object creation mechanisms, trying to create objects in a manner suitable to the situation.
  - o Examples: Singleton, Factory, Abstract Factory, Builder, Prototype

- **Structural Patterns**: These patterns deal with object composition or how to combine classes and objects to form larger structures.
  - o Examples: Adapter, Decorator, Proxy, Composite, Flyweight, Facade
- **Behavioral Patterns**: These patterns focus on communication between objects, what goes on between objects and how they operate together.
  - o Examples: Strategy, Command, Observer, Chain of Responsibility, State, Visitor

In this chapter, we will focus on the **Strategy**, **Command**, and **Proxy** design patterns, which are all behavioral and structural patterns that help solve common problems in software development.

Strategy, Command, and Proxy Patterns

- **Strategy Pattern**: The **Strategy pattern** allows a client to choose an algorithm at runtime. It defines a family of algorithms and makes them interchangeable. This is useful when you want to define different variations of an algorithm and decide which one to use dynamically.
  - o **Example**: A sorting strategy where you could choose between different sorting algorithms (e.g., quicksort, mergesort, bubble sort).

o **Implementation**:

```java
// Strategy Interface
interface SortStrategy {
    void sort(int[] array);
}

// Concrete Strategy 1
class QuickSort implements SortStrategy {
    @Override
    public void sort(int[] array) {

System.out.println("QuickSort algorithm");
        // Implement quicksort algorithm here
    }
}

// Concrete Strategy 2
class MergeSort implements SortStrategy {
    @Override
    public void sort(int[] array) {

System.out.println("MergeSort algorithm");
```

```
            //    Implement    mergesort
algorithm here
    }
}


// Context Class
class Sorter {
    private SortStrategy strategy;

    public        Sorter(SortStrategy
strategy) {
        this.strategy = strategy;
    }

    public                      void
setStrategy(SortStrategy strategy) {
        this.strategy = strategy;
    }

    public   void   sortArray(int[]
array) {
        strategy.sort(array);
    }
}

public class Main {
    public static void main(String[]
args) {
        int[] array = {5, 2, 8, 1};
```

```
        Sorter    sorter    =    new
Sorter(new QuickSort());
        sorter.sortArray(array);  //
Output: QuickSort algorithm

        sorter.setStrategy(new
MergeSort());
        sorter.sortArray(array);  //
Output: MergeSort algorithm
    }
}
```

- **Command Pattern**: The **Command pattern** encapsulates a request as an object, allowing users to parameterize clients with queues, requests, and operations. It decouples the sender of the request from the object that executes the request, making it useful for undo/redo functionality, queues, or batch processing.
    - **Example**: In a text editor, you might use commands like "", "paste", "undo", and "redo".
    - **Implementation**:

    java

```java
// Command Interface
interface Command {
    void execute();
}
```

```java
// Concrete Command: Turn On Light
class TurnOnLightCommand implements
Command {
    private Light light;

    public  TurnOnLightCommand(Light
light) {
        this.light = light;
    }

    @Override
    public void execute() {
        light.turnOn();
    }
}

// Concrete Command: Turn Off Light
class TurnOffLightCommand implements
Command {
    private Light light;

    public TurnOffLightCommand(Light
light) {
        this.light = light;
    }

    @Override
    public void execute() {
```

```java
        light.turnOff();
    }
}


// Receiver Class
class Light {
    public void turnOn() {
        System.out.println("Light is
ON");
    }

    public void turnOff() {
        System.out.println("Light is
OFF");
    }
}

// Invoker Class
class RemoteControl {
    private Command command;

    public void setCommand(Command
command) {
        this.command = command;
    }

    public void pressButton() {
        command.execute();
    }
```

```
}

public class Main {
    public static void main(String[]
args) {
        Light livingRoomLight = new
Light();

        Command turnOnLight = new
TurnOnLightCommand(livingRoomLight)
;
        Command turnOffLight = new
TurnOffLightCommand(livingRoomLight
);

        RemoteControl remote = new
RemoteControl();

remote.setCommand(turnOnLight);
        remote.pressButton();     //
Output: Light is ON


remote.setCommand(turnOffLight);
        remote.pressButton();     //
Output: Light is OFF
    }
}
```

113

- **Proxy Pattern**: The **Proxy pattern** provides an object representing another object. It acts as a surrogate or placeholder for another object, controlling access to it. Proxies are often used for lazy initialization, access control, logging, or caching.

  o **Example**: A virtual proxy that handles loading a large image only when necessary.

  o **Implementation**:

```java
// Subject Interface
interface RealSubject {
    void request();
}

// RealSubject: The actual object
class RealSubjectImpl implements
RealSubject {
    @Override
    public void request() {

System.out.println("RealSubject:
Handling request");
    }
}

// Proxy: Controls access to the
RealSubject
```

114

```java
class Proxy implements RealSubject {
    private          RealSubjectImpl
realSubject;

    @Override
    public void request() {
        if (realSubject == null) {
            realSubject     =     new
RealSubjectImpl();        //    Lazy
initialization
        }
        realSubject.request();
    }
}

public class Main {
    public static void main(String[]
args) {
        RealSubject    proxy    =    new
Proxy();
        proxy.request();  // Output:
RealSubject: Handling request
    }
}
```

Implementing Design Patterns in Java

Implementing design patterns in Java involves creating appropriate interfaces, abstract classes, or concrete implementations based on the specific pattern. By understanding the intent of the design pattern and the problem it solves, developers can choose the right pattern to structure their code.

- **Steps for Implementation**:
    1. **Identify the Problem**: Understand the problem and determine if a design pattern is a good fit.
    2. **Select the Appropriate Pattern**: Choose the pattern that best solves the problem. Each pattern addresses specific problems related to object creation, composition, or behavior.
    3. **Define Interfaces or Classes**: Depending on the pattern, create abstract classes or interfaces to define common behaviors.
    4. **Provide Concrete Implementations**: Implement the pattern with concrete classes that fulfill the defined behavior.
    5. **Integrate the Pattern into Your Application**: Use the pattern to solve the specific problem in your application, ensuring flexibility, maintainability, and reusability.

Real-World Example: Refactoring an Application with Design Patterns

Let's consider a simple example of a shopping cart application. Initially, the cart class might be a large, monolithic class responsible for various operations like adding items, calculating total price, applying discounts, and processing payments. Refactoring this class with design patterns can improve code readability, maintainability, and flexibility.

- **Step 1: Refactor with the Strategy Pattern**: Use the **Strategy pattern** to separate different discount strategies. For example, a regular discount, seasonal discount, or promotional discount.

```java
java

// DiscountStrategy Interface
interface DiscountStrategy {
    double applyDiscount(double price);
}

// Concrete Strategy 1: Regular Discount
class RegularDiscount implements DiscountStrategy {
    @Override
    public double applyDiscount(double price) {
```

117

```java
        return price * 0.9;    // 10%
discount
    }
}


// Concrete Strategy 2: Seasonal Discount
class     SeasonalDiscount     implements
DiscountStrategy {
    @Override
    public   double   applyDiscount(double
price) {
        return price * 0.8;    // 20%
discount
    }
}


// Context Class: ShoppingCart
class ShoppingCart {
    private              DiscountStrategy
discountStrategy;


    public                          void
setDiscountStrategy(DiscountStrategy
discountStrategy) {
        this.discountStrategy          =
discountStrategy;
    }
```

```java
    public                          double
calculateTotalPrice(double price) {
        return
discountStrategy.applyDiscount(price);
    }
}


public class Main {
    public static void main(String[] args)
{
        ShoppingCart    cart    =    new
ShoppingCart();

        cart.setDiscountStrategy(new
RegularDiscount());
        System.out.println("Price    after
discount:              "              +
cart.calculateTotalPrice(100));

        cart.setDiscountStrategy(new
SeasonalDiscount());
        System.out.println("Price    after
discount:              "              +
cart.calculateTotalPrice(100));
    }
}
```

- **Step 2: Command Pattern for Operations**: Use the **Command pattern** to separate various operations, such

119

as adding items, applying discounts, and processing payments, so that each action can be executed independently and can support undo/redo functionality.

```java
interface Command {
    void execute();
}

class AddItemCommand implements Command {
    private ShoppingCart cart;
    private String item;

    public      AddItemCommand(ShoppingCart
cart, String item) {
        this.cart = cart;
        this.item = item;
    }

    @Override
    public void execute() {
        cart.addItem(item);  // Add item to
cart
    }
}

// Invoker class (e.g., Controller)
class CartController {
```

```java
    private Command command;

    public      void      setCommand(Command
command) {
        this.command = command;
    }

    public void pressButton() {
        command.execute();
    }
}
```

This chapter explored how to use the **Strategy**, **Command**, and **Proxy** design patterns to improve the structure of your applications. By implementing these patterns, you can increase flexibility, maintainability, and scalability. We also demonstrated how to refactor an application, such as a shopping cart system, to make it more modular and easier to extend in the future. In the next chapter, we will explore how to handle Java I/O operations to read and write files efficiently.

CHAPTER 10

JAVA I/O AND FILE HANDLING

In this chapter, we will explore Java's **I/O (Input/Output)** system, which provides a rich set of APIs for reading from and writing to files, directories, and streams. Understanding file handling is crucial for building applications that need to persist data or interact with the file system. We will also cover **buffered I/O** and **serialization**, two essential techniques for optimizing file reading/writing and storing objects in files.

Introduction to Java I/O Streams

Java provides a comprehensive I/O API for handling data between a program and external systems such as files, network connections, or memory. The core idea in Java I/O is based on streams.

- **Stream Types**:
    1. **Byte Streams**: These deal with raw binary data (e.g., `FileInputStream`, `FileOutputStream`). They are used for reading and writing binary data such as image files, audio files, or any non-text data.

2. **Character Streams**: These deal with character data, converting bytes to characters using a character encoding (e.g., `FileReader`, `FileWriter`). They are typically used for reading and writing text files.

Both byte and character streams implement the `InputStream` and `OutputStream` classes, which are the foundational classes for byte streams, and the `Reader` and `Writer` classes for character streams.

- **Basic I/O Operations**:
  - o **Input**: Reading data from a source (e.g., reading a file).
  - o **Output**: Writing data to a destination (e.g., writing to a file).

Example (Reading a Text File):

```java

import java.io.FileReader;
import java.io.BufferedReader;
import java.io.IOException;

public class ReadFile {
    public static void main(String[] args)
{
```

```
        try (BufferedReader reader = new
BufferedReader(new
FileReader("example.txt"))) {
            String line;
            while           ((line      =
reader.readLine()) != null) {
                System.out.println(line);
            }
        } catch (IOException e) {
            e.printStackTrace();
        }
    }
}
```

In this example, `FileReader` reads data from a text file, and `BufferedReader` provides an efficient way to read data line by line.

File and Directory Operations

Java's `java.nio.file` package, introduced in Java 7, provides an efficient and flexible way to work with files and directories. You can perform various operations such as creating, deleting, renaming, and ing files or directories.

- **Basic File Operations**:
    - o **Creating a File**: You can create a file using the `Files.createFile()` method.

```java

import java.nio.file.Files;
import java.nio.file.Path;
import java.nio.file.Paths;
import java.io.IOException;

public class CreateFile {
    public static void main(String[] args) {
        Path path = Paths.get("newfile.txt");
        try {
            Files.createFile(path);

System.out.println("File created: " + path.toString());
        } catch (IOException e) {
            e.printStackTrace();
        }
    }
}
```

o **Creating a Directory**:

```java

Path dirPath = Paths.get("newDirectory");
try {
```

125

```
Files.createDirectory(dirPath);
System.out.println("Directory
created: " + dirPath.toString());
} catch (IOException e) {
    e.printStackTrace();
}
```

o **Listing Directory Contents**:

java

```
import
java.nio.file.DirectoryStream;
import java.nio.file.Files;
import java.nio.file.Path;
import java.nio.file.Paths;

public class ListFiles {
    public static void main(String[]
args) {
        Path         dirPath      =
Paths.get("someDirectory");
        try    (DirectoryStream<Path>
stream                           =
Files.newDirectoryStream(dirPath)) {
            for   (Path   entry   :
stream) {

System.out.println(entry.getFileNam
e());
```

```
            }
        } catch (IOException e) {
            e.printStackTrace();
        }
    }
}
```

o **ing and Deleting Files**:

```java
Path              source              =
Paths.get("source.txt");
Path            destination            =
Paths.get("destination.txt");
try {
    Files.(source, destination);
    System.out.println("File   copied
successfully.");

    Files.delete(destination);     //
Deletes the copied file
    System.out.println("File deleted
successfully.");
} catch (IOException e) {
    e.printStackTrace();
}
```

Buffered I/O and Serialization

- **Buffered I/O**: Buffered I/O streams improve the performance of file reading and writing by reducing the number of disk access operations. The `BufferedReader` and `BufferedWriter` classes provide a buffered version of character streams, and the `BufferedInputStream` and `BufferedOutputStream` classes do the same for byte streams.

  o **Example (Buffered Input and Output)**:

  ```java
  import java.io.BufferedReader;
  import java.io.FileReader;
  import java.io.FileWriter;
  import java.io.BufferedWriter;
  import java.io.IOException;

  public class BufferedIOExample {
      public static void main(String[]
  args) {
          try (BufferedReader reader =
  new             BufferedReader(new
  FileReader("input.txt"));
              BufferedWriter writer =
  new             BufferedWriter(new
  FileWriter("output.txt"))) {
              String line;
  ```

128

```
            while        ((line     =
reader.readLine()) != null) {
              writer.write(line);
              writer.newLine();
// Add newline between lines
          }
      } catch (IOException e) {
          e.printStackTrace();
      }
   }
}
```

- o In this example, `BufferedReader` reads data efficiently from a file, and `BufferedWriter` writes the data to a new file. This is much faster than reading and writing data byte by byte or character by character.

- **Serialization**: Serialization is the process of converting an object into a byte stream, which can then be saved to a file or sent over a network. In Java, an object can be serialized using the `Serializable` interface and the `ObjectOutputStream/ObjectInputStream` classes.

  - o **Example (Serialization and Deserialization)**:

    ```
    java

    import java.io.Serializable;
    import java.io.FileOutputStream;
    ```

```java
import java.io.ObjectOutputStream;
import java.io.FileInputStream;
import java.io.ObjectInputStream;
import java.io.IOException;

class Person implements Serializable
{
    private String name;
    private int age;

    public Person(String name, int
age) {
        this.name = name;
        this.age = age;
    }

    @Override
    public String toString() {
        return    "Person{name='"    +
name + "', age=" + age + "}";
    }
}

public class SerializationExample {
    public static void main(String[]
args) {
        // Serialize object to a file
        Person    person    =    new
Person("John", 30);
```

```java
        try (ObjectOutputStream out
=    new    ObjectOutputStream(new
FileOutputStream("person.ser"))) {

out.writeObject(person);

System.out.println("Object
serialized to person.ser");
        } catch (IOException e) {
            e.printStackTrace();
        }

        // Deserialize object from a
file
        try (ObjectInputStream in =
new            ObjectInputStream(new
FileInputStream("person.ser"))) {
            Person
deserializedPerson    =    (Person)
in.readObject();

System.out.println("Deserialized
object: " + deserializedPerson);
        } catch (IOException |
ClassNotFoundException e) {
            e.printStackTrace();
        }
    }
}
```

- In this example, the `Person` object is serialized to a file and later deserialized back into a Java object. This allows objects to be easily saved to and loaded from storage.

Real-World Example: Creating a File Importer and Exporter for a System

In this real-world example, we'll build a simple file importer and exporter system that reads data from a CSV file, processes it, and then exports the processed data into a new file. This could be useful in business applications for importing and exporting customer data or transaction records.

- **Step 1: Define a Data Model (e.g., Customer)**: First, let's define a simple `Customer` class.

```java
class Customer {
    private String name;
    private int age;

    public Customer(String name, int age) {
        this.name = name;
        this.age = age;
    }
```

```java
public String getName() {
    return name;
}

public int getAge() {
    return age;
}

@Override
public String toString() {
    return "Customer{name='" + name +
"', age=" + age + "}";
}
}
```

- **Step 2: Create the File Importer**: The importer will read customer data from a CSV file, parse the data, and store it in a list.

```java
import java.io.BufferedReader;
import java.io.FileReader;
import java.io.IOException;
import java.util.ArrayList;
import java.util.List;

public class FileImporter {
```

```java
public                    List<Customer>
importCustomers(String fileName) {
        List<Customer>   customers   =   new
ArrayList<>();
        try (BufferedReader  reader  =  new
BufferedReader(new  FileReader(fileName)))
{
            String line;
            while           ((line       =
reader.readLine()) != null) {
                String[]      data      =
line.split(",");
                String name = data[0];
                int            age       =
Integer.parseInt(data[1]);
                customers.add(new
Customer(name, age));
            }
        } catch (IOException e) {
            e.printStackTrace();
        }
        return customers;
    }
}
```

- **Step 3: Create the File Exporter**: The exporter will write the customer data to a new CSV file.

```
java
```

```java
import java.io.BufferedWriter;
import java.io.FileWriter;
import java.io.IOException;
import java.util.List;

public class FileExporter {
    public                           void
exportCustomers(List<Customer>  customers,
String fileName) {
        try (BufferedWriter writer = new
BufferedWriter(new  FileWriter(fileName)))
{
            for  (Customer  customer  :
customers) {

writer.write(customer.getName()  +  ","  +
customer.getAge());
                writer.newLine();
            }
        } catch (IOException e) {
            e.printStackTrace();
        }
    }
}
```

- **Step 4: Demonstrating the Import and Export Functionality**: Finally, we'll test the importer and exporter by reading data from a CSV file and then exporting it to a new file.

135

```java
public class Main {
    public static void main(String[] args)
{
        FileImporter importer = new
FileImporter();
        FileExporter exporter = new
FileExporter();

        List<Customer> customers =
importer.importCustomers("customers.csv")
;
        System.out.println("Imported
customers: " + customers);


        exporter.exportCustomers(customers,
"exported_customers.csv");
        System.out.println("Customers
exported to exported_customers.csv");
    }
}
```

This chapter covered the core concepts of **Java I/O** and file handling, including working with streams, file and directory operations, buffered I/O, and serialization. We also provided a real-world example of a file importer and exporter system that reads data from a file, processes it, and exports it back. Understanding how to handle files and directories efficiently is crucial for developing data-driven applications. In the next chapter, we will explore more advanced Java features such as multithreading and concurrency.

CHAPTER 11

NETWORKING AND SOCKETS IN JAVA

In this chapter, we will explore how Java enables communication between devices over a network. Networking is a critical aspect of modern applications, from simple file transfers to complex client-server systems. We will cover the basics of networking in Java, how to work with sockets, and the different communication protocols like HTTP, TCP/IP, and UDP. Finally, we will build a real-world chat application using Java networking to demonstrate these concepts.

Basics of Networking in Java

Networking in Java allows programs to communicate over the internet or within a local area network (LAN). Java provides a rich API for working with networking, which is encapsulated in the `java.net` package. The core concept of networking in Java is based on **sockets**, which provide endpoints for communication between two machines.

- **Sockets**: A socket is a communication endpoint that allows for the sending and receiving of data over a network. It can either be a **server socket** (waiting for incoming connections) or a **client socket** (connecting to a server).

- **IP Address and Port**: Each machine in a network is identified by an **IP address**. An **IP address** is a unique identifier for devices on the network. Ports allow multiple applications to use the network simultaneously. Each port is identified by a number, with commonly used ports (e.g., port 80 for HTTP, port 443 for HTTPS) reserved for specific protocols.

- **TCP and UDP**:
  - **TCP (Transmission Control Protocol)**: TCP is a connection-oriented protocol that ensures reliable data transmission. It guarantees that data sent from one machine will reach the other machine in the correct order and without loss.
  - **UDP (User Datagram Protocol)**: UDP is a connectionless protocol. It does not guarantee delivery or order of packets, making it faster but less reliable than TCP.

Working with Sockets and Client-Server Architecture

Java provides a simple way to work with both TCP and UDP sockets using classes in the `java.net` package. Let's discuss the basic concepts of **client-server architecture** and how to implement socket-based communication in Java.

- **Client-Server Architecture**: In this architecture, one machine (the server) waits for incoming requests from other machines (clients). The server listens on a specific port for requests, and the client connects to the server to send or receive data. The server and client communicate using sockets.

- **Creating a Server Socket**: The ServerSocket class in Java is used to create a server-side socket that listens for incoming client connections.

  o **Example**:

```java

import java.net.ServerSocket;
import java.net.Socket;
import java.io.IOException;

public class Server {
    public static void main(String[]
args) {
        try            (ServerSocket
serverSocket        =        new
ServerSocket(1234)) {
```

```
System.out.println("Server        is
listening on port 1234...");

        while (true) {
            // Accept  client
connections
            Socket  clientSocket
= serverSocket.accept();

System.out.println("New        client
connected:           "           +
clientSocket.getInetAddress().getHo
stName());

                // Handle  client
communication in a new thread (for
simplicity, we'll not go into that
here)
        }
    } catch (IOException e) {
        e.printStackTrace();
    }
    }
}
```

- In this example, the server is listening on port 1234 for incoming client connections. Once a client connects, the server accepts the connection and can begin communicating with the client.

- **Creating a Client Socket**: The client side uses the `Socket` class to connect to the server and communicate over the network.

  o **Example**:

```java
import java.net.Socket;
import java.io.IOException;

public class Client {
    public static void main(String[] args) {
        try (Socket socket = new Socket("localhost", 1234)) {

            System.out.println("Connected to the server at localhost on port 1234");

            // Send and receive data with the server here
        } catch (IOException e) {
            e.printStackTrace();
        }
    }
}
```

- Here, the client connects to the server running on `localhost` (the local machine) on port 1234. Once the connection is established, the client can start communicating with the server.

Protocols: HTTP, TCP/IP, and UDP

- **HTTP (Hypertext Transfer Protocol)**: HTTP is the protocol used for transferring web pages on the internet. It is a text-based protocol and works over TCP. HTTP is stateless, meaning each request from a client to a server is treated as an independent transaction.

    o Java provides the `HttpURLConnection` class for working with HTTP requests and responses.

Example (HTTP Client in Java):

```java
java

import java.io.BufferedReader;
import java.io.InputStreamReader;
import java.net.HttpURLConnection;
import java.net.URL;

public class HttpClient {
    public static void main(String[] args)
{
```

```
        try {
            URL         url       =        new
URL("http://example.com");
                HttpURLConnection connection =
(HttpURLConnection) url.openConnection();

connection.setRequestMethod("GET");

                BufferedReader reader = new
BufferedReader(new
InputStreamReader(connection.getInputStre
am()));
            String line;
            while           ((line         =
reader.readLine()) != null) {
                System.out.println(line);
            }
            reader.close();
        } catch (Exception e) {
            e.printStackTrace();
        }
    }
}
```

- **TCP/IP**: TCP/IP is a set of protocols used to govern how data is sent over the internet or a local network. TCP is responsible for ensuring reliable data transmission, while IP handles the routing and addressing of data.

- **UDP**: UDP is a lightweight, connectionless protocol used for sending data without ensuring reliability. It is often used for applications that require low-latency communication, such as real-time video or voice streaming.

    o **Example (UDP Server and Client)**:

    ```java
    // UDP Server
    import java.net.DatagramPacket;
    import java.net.DatagramSocket;
    import java.net.SocketException;

    public class UDPServer {
        public static void main(String[]
    args) throws Exception {
            DatagramSocket socket = new
    DatagramSocket(1234);
            byte[] buffer = new
    byte[1024];
            DatagramPacket packet = new
    DatagramPacket(buffer,
    buffer.length);

            while (true) {
                socket.receive(packet);
    // Receive message
    ```

145

```
        String  message  =  new
String(packet.getData(),        0,
packet.getLength());

System.out.println("Received:  "  +
message);
        }
    }
}


// UDP Client
import java.net.DatagramPacket;
import java.net.DatagramSocket;

public class UDPClient {
    public static void main(String[]
args) throws Exception {
        DatagramSocket socket = new
DatagramSocket();
        String message = "Hello, UDP
Server!";
        byte[]        buffer        =
message.getBytes();
        DatagramPacket packet = new
DatagramPacket(buffer,
buffer.length,

java.net.InetAddress.getByName("loc
alhost"), 1234);
```

```
        socket.send(packet);        //
Send message
        socket.close();
    }
}
```

Real-World Example: Building a Chat Application with Java Networking

In this section, we will implement a simple **chat application** where multiple clients can connect to a server and send messages to each other in real-time.

- **Step 1: The Server**: The server will listen for incoming client connections, accept them, and broadcast messages to all connected clients.

```java
import java.io.*;
import java.net.*;
import java.util.*;

public class ChatServer {
    private    static    Set<PrintWriter>
clientWriters = new HashSet<>();
```

```java
    public static void main(String[] args)
{
        System.out.println("Chat        Server
started...");
        try (ServerSocket serverSocket =
new ServerSocket(1234)) {
            while (true) {
                new
ClientHandler(serverSocket.accept()).star
t();
            }
        } catch (IOException e) {
            e.printStackTrace();
        }
    }


    private static class ClientHandler
extends Thread {
        private Socket socket;
        private PrintWriter out;
        private BufferedReader in;

        public          ClientHandler(Socket
socket) {
            this.socket = socket;
        }

        @Override
        public void run() {
```

```
        try {
            in          =          new
BufferedReader(new
InputStreamReader(socket.getInputStream()
));
            out         =          new
PrintWriter(socket.getOutputStream(),
true);
            synchronized
(clientWriters) {

clientWriters.add(out);
            }

            String message;
            while       ((message     =
in.readLine()) != null) {
                synchronized
(clientWriters) {
                    for    (PrintWriter
writer : clientWriters) {

writer.println(message);
                    }
                }
            }
        } catch (IOException e) {
            e.printStackTrace();
        } finally {
```

149

```
                    try {
                        socket.close();
                    } catch (IOException e) {
                        e.printStackTrace();
                    }
                    synchronized
(clientWriters) {

clientWriters.remove(out);
                    }
                }
            }
        }
}
```

- **Step 2: The Client**: The client will connect to the server and allow the user to send messages. It will also listen for messages from other clients and display them.

```java

import java.io.*;
import java.net.*;

public class ChatClient {
    public static void main(String[] args)
{
        try (Socket socket = new
Socket("localhost", 1234);
```

```java
            BufferedReader  reader  =  new
BufferedReader(new
InputStreamReader(socket.getInputStream()
));
            PrintWriter   writer   =   new
PrintWriter(socket.getOutputStream(),
true);
            BufferedReader   userInput   =
new                     BufferedReader(new
InputStreamReader(System.in))) {

            // Read  messages  from  other
clients
            new Thread(() -> {
                try {
                    String message;
                    while  ((message  =
reader.readLine()) != null) {

System.out.println(message);
                    }
                } catch (IOException e) {
                    e.printStackTrace();
                }
            }).start();

            // Send messages to the server
            String userMessage;
```

151

```
        while       ((userMessage      =
userInput.readLine()) != null) {

writer.println(userMessage);
            }
        } catch (IOException e) {
            e.printStackTrace();
        }
    }
}
```

In this chat application:

- The **server** listens for client connections on port 1234 and broadcasts any incoming messages to all connected clients.
- Each **client** connects to the server, sends messages, and displays any messages received from other clients.

This chapter covered the basics of **Java networking** using **sockets** and how to implement client-server applications. We explored various protocols such as **HTTP**, **TCP/IP**, and **UDP**, and saw a real-world example of building a chat application. Networking is an essential skill for creating distributed applications, and mastering these concepts will help you build robust, scalable networked systems. In the next chapter, we will discuss **Java database connectivity (JDBC)** for interacting with relational databases.

CHAPTER 12

DATABASE CONNECTIVITY WITH JDBC

In this chapter, we will explore **Java Database Connectivity (JDBC)**, which provides a standard API for connecting Java applications to relational databases. JDBC allows you to interact with databases, execute queries, and perform CRUD (Create, Read, Update, Delete) operations. We will cover the basics of JDBC, including connecting to databases, executing SQL queries, and using **Prepared Statements** for secure and efficient database operations. We will also build a real-world example of a **data management system** using JDBC.

Introduction to JDBC (Java Database Connectivity)

JDBC (Java Database Connectivity) is an API in Java that allows you to connect and interact with relational databases such as MySQL, PostgreSQL, SQLite, and Oracle. JDBC provides a set of classes and interfaces for executing SQL queries and managing database connections.

The key components of JDBC are:

1. **JDBC Drivers**: JDBC drivers are platform-specific implementations that allow Java applications to connect to a specific database.

2. **Connection**: The `Connection` interface represents the database connection.

3. **Statement**: The `Statement` interface allows you to execute SQL queries.

4. **ResultSet**: The `ResultSet` interface holds the data returned by executing a query.

5. **PreparedStatement**: A more secure and efficient way to execute SQL queries, especially for queries with user input.

JDBC operates through the following sequence of steps:

1. **Establishing a connection** to the database.

2. **Creating a statement** to execute SQL queries.

3. **Executing the query** (e.g., SELECT, INSERT, UPDATE, DELETE).

4. **Processing the results** (e.g., reading data from `ResultSet`).

5. **Closing the connection**.

155

Connecting to Relational Databases (SQL)

The first step in JDBC is to establish a connection to a database. JDBC provides the `DriverManager` class to load the appropriate JDBC driver and establish the connection.

- **Steps for Establishing a Connection**:
    1. Load the database driver.
    2. Use the `DriverManager.getConnection()` method to connect to the database using a JDBC URL, username, and password.
    3. Once the connection is established, you can begin executing SQL queries.
- **Example: Connecting to MySQL Database**:

```java

import java.sql.Connection;
import java.sql.DriverManager;
import java.sql.SQLException;

public class DatabaseConnection {
    public static void main(String[] args)
{
        // Database URL, username, and
password
        String                url              =
"jdbc:mysql://localhost:3306/mydatabase";
```

```
        String user = "root";
        String password = "password";

        try {
            // Load the MySQL JDBC driver

Class.forName("com.mysql.cj.jdbc.Driver")
;

            // Establish the connection
            Connection      connection      =
DriverManager.getConnection(url,      user,
password);
            System.out.println("Connected
to the database successfully!");

            // Close the connection
            connection.close();
        } catch (ClassNotFoundException |
SQLException e) {
            e.printStackTrace();
        }
    }
}
```

In this example, we use
DriverManager.getConnection() to connect to a
MySQL database. The URL specifies the database
location (localhost), the database name

157

(mydatabase), and login credentials (root and password).

CRUD Operations and Prepared Statements

JDBC allows you to execute SQL queries for performing CRUD operations on a database. These operations are:

- **Create**: Insert data into the database.
- **Read**: Retrieve data from the database.
- **Update**: Modify existing data in the database.
- **Delete**: Remove data from the database.
- **Statement vs PreparedStatement**:
  - ○ **Statement**: Used for simple SQL queries without parameters. It is vulnerable to SQL injection attacks if user input is not sanitized.
  - ○ **PreparedStatement**: Used for executing SQL queries with parameters. It is more secure and efficient because it pre-compiles the SQL statement and allows for parameterized queries.

Create (Insert) Operation with PreparedStatement:

java

```
import java.sql.Connection;
import java.sql.DriverManager;
import java.sql.PreparedStatement;
```

```java
import java.sql.SQLException;

public class CreateExample {
    public static void main(String[] args) {
        String url = "jdbc:mysql://localhost:3306/mydatabase";
        String user = "root";
        String password = "password";
        String query = "INSERT INTO customers (name, email) VALUES (?, ?)";

        try (Connection connection = DriverManager.getConnection(url, user, password);
             PreparedStatement statement = connection.prepareStatement(query)) {

            // Set parameters
            statement.setString(1, "John Doe");
            statement.setString(2, "johndoe@example.com");

            // Execute the insert query
            int rowsAffected = statement.executeUpdate();
            System.out.println("Rows affected: " + rowsAffected);
        } catch (SQLException e) {
            e.printStackTrace();
```

```
        }
    }
}
```

In this example, we use `PreparedStatement` to insert a new customer into the `customers` table. The `?` placeholders are replaced with actual values (`"John Doe"` and `"johndoe@example.com"`).

Read (Select) Operation with ResultSet:
java

```java
import java.sql.*;

public class ReadExample {
    public static void main(String[] args) {
        String url = "jdbc:mysql://localhost:3306/mydatabase";
        String user = "root";
        String password = "password";
        String query = "SELECT id, name, email FROM customers";

        try (Connection connection = DriverManager.getConnection(url, user, password);
            Statement statement = connection.createStatement();
```

```
            ResultSet        resultSet      =
statement.executeQuery(query)) {


        // Process the result set
        while (resultSet.next()) {
            int id = resultSet.getInt("id");
            String          name           =
resultSet.getString("name");
            String          email          =
resultSet.getString("email");
            System.out.println(id + ": " +
name + " - " + email);
        }
    } catch (SQLException e) {
        e.printStackTrace();
    }
    }
}
```

In this example, we use a `Statement` to execute a `SELECT` query and process the `ResultSet` to retrieve and display the data.

Update Operation:
java

```
import java.sql.*;

public class UpdateExample {
    public static void main(String[] args) {
```

```java
        String              url              =
"jdbc:mysql://localhost:3306/mydatabase";
        String user = "root";
        String password = "password";
        String query = "UPDATE customers SET
email = ? WHERE id = ?";

        try      (Connection     connection      =
DriverManager.getConnection(url,              user,
password);
            PreparedStatement    statement      =
connection.prepareStatement(query)) {

            // Set parameters
            statement.setString(1,
"newemail@example.com");
            statement.setInt(2, 1);    // Update
customer with id 1

            // Execute the update query
            int           rowsAffected          =
statement.executeUpdate();
            System.out.println("Rows affected: "
+ rowsAffected);
        } catch (SQLException e) {
            e.printStackTrace();
        }
    }
}
```

162

Delete Operation:

java

```java
import java.sql.*;

public class DeleteExample {
    public static void main(String[] args) {
        String                    url                    =
"jdbc:mysql://localhost:3306/mydatabase";
        String user = "root";
        String password = "password";
        String  query  =  "DELETE  FROM  customers
WHERE id = ?";

        try    (Connection    connection    =
DriverManager.getConnection(url,              user,
password);
            PreparedStatement    statement    =
connection.prepareStatement(query)) {

            // Set parameter
            statement.setInt(1, 1);   // Delete
customer with id 1

            // Execute the delete query
            int         rowsAffected         =
statement.executeUpdate();
            System.out.println("Rows affected: "
+ rowsAffected);
```

```
    } catch (SQLException e) {
        e.printStackTrace();
    }
  }
}
```

Real-World Example: Building a Java-based Data Management System

Let's put everything together by building a simple **data management system** for storing and managing customer information using JDBC. This system will allow users to add, view, update, and delete customer records.

- **Step 1: Define a Customer Class**:

```java
java

public class Customer {
    private int id;
    private String name;
    private String email;

    public Customer(int id, String name,
String email) {
        this.id = id;
        this.name = name;
        this.email = email;
```

164

```java
    }

    public int getId() {
        return id;
    }

    public String getName() {
        return name;
    }

    public String getEmail() {
        return email;
    }

    @Override
    public String toString() {
        return "Customer{id=" + id + ",
name='" + name + "', email='" + email +
"'}";
    }
}
```

- **Step 2: Create a DataManager Class**: This class will handle CRUD operations for managing customer data.

```java
java

import java.sql.*;
import java.util.*;
```

```java
public class DataManager {
    private Connection connection;

    public DataManager(String url, String user, String password) throws SQLException {
        this.connection = DriverManager.getConnection(url, user, password);
    }

    // Add a customer
    public void addCustomer(Customer customer) throws SQLException {
        String query = "INSERT INTO customers (name, email) VALUES (?, ?)";
        try (PreparedStatement statement = connection.prepareStatement(query)) {
            statement.setString(1, customer.getName());
            statement.setString(2, customer.getEmail());
            statement.executeUpdate();
        }
    }

    // Get all customers
    public List<Customer> getAllCustomers() throws SQLException {
```

166

```java
        List<Customer> customers = new
ArrayList<>();
        String query = "SELECT id, name,
email FROM customers";
        try (Statement statement =
connection.createStatement();
            ResultSet resultSet =
statement.executeQuery(query)) {

            while (resultSet.next()) {
                int id =
resultSet.getInt("id");
                String name =
resultSet.getString("name");
                String email =
resultSet.getString("email");
                customers.add(new
Customer(id, name, email));
            }
        }
        return customers;
    }


    // Update customer
    public void updateCustomer(int id,
String newEmail) throws SQLException {
        String query = "UPDATE customers
SET email = ? WHERE id = ?";
```

```
        try (PreparedStatement statement =
connection.prepareStatement(query)) {
            statement.setString(1,
newEmail);
            statement.setInt(2, id);
            statement.executeUpdate();
        }
    }


    // Delete customer
    public void deleteCustomer(int id)
throws SQLException {
        String query = "DELETE FROM
customers WHERE id = ?";
        try (PreparedStatement statement =
connection.prepareStatement(query)) {
            statement.setInt(1, id);
            statement.executeUpdate();
        }
    }
}
```

- **Step 3: Using the DataManager in the Main Application**:

```
java

public class Main {
    public static void main(String[] args)
{
```

```
    try {
        DataManager dataManager = new
DataManager("jdbc:mysql://localhost:3306/
mydatabase", "root", "password");

        // Add new customer
        dataManager.addCustomer(new
Customer(0,          "John          Doe",
"johndoe@example.com"));

        // Retrieve and display all
customers
        List<Customer>   customers   =
dataManager.getAllCustomers();

customers.forEach(System.out::println);

        // Update a customer's email
        dataManager.updateCustomer(1,
"newemail@example.com");

        // Delete a customer

dataManager.deleteCustomer(2);

    } catch (SQLException e) {
        e.printStackTrace();
    }
}
```

```
}
```

In this example, the `DataManager` class handles all CRUD operations, and the main application demonstrates how to use these operations.

This chapter covered the essentials of **Java Database Connectivity (JDBC)**, including how to connect to relational databases, perform CRUD operations, and use **PreparedStatement** for secure querying. We also built a real-world **data management system** to help you understand how to interact with a database from a Java application. In the next chapter, we will explore **multithreading** and **concurrency** in Java to handle parallel tasks efficiently.

CHAPTER 13

JAVA WEB DEVELOPMENT OVERVIEW

In this chapter, we will provide an overview of **Java Web Development**, introducing essential web technologies, including **Servlets** and **JSP (JavaServer Pages)**. We will also explore popular Java-based web frameworks such as **Spring**, **JSF (JavaServer Faces)**, and **Struts**, and provide a real-world example of building a **simple web-based task manager**. Web development in Java allows you to build dynamic, scalable, and robust applications, and this chapter will help you get started with the fundamental concepts.

Introduction to Java Web Technologies

Java provides a rich ecosystem of technologies for building web applications. The main components include:

- **Servlets**: Java Servlets are server-side programs that handle HTTP requests and generate dynamic web content (HTML, JSON, etc.). They form the core of Java-based web applications.

- **JSP (JavaServer Pages)**: JSP is a technology used to create dynamically generated web pages based on HTML, XML, or other document types. JSP allows you to embed Java code directly into HTML pages, making it easier to create dynamic content.

- **Web Containers/Servers**: A web container (or servlet container) is a part of a web server that interacts with Java Servlets and JSPs. Examples include **Apache Tomcat**, **Jetty**, and **JBoss**.

- **HTTP Protocol**: Web applications primarily use the HTTP protocol for communication between clients (web browsers) and servers.

Setting Up a Simple Web Application with Servlets and JSP

In this section, we'll walk through setting up a simple Java web application using **Servlets** and **JSPs**. We will use **Apache Tomcat** as our web server.

Step 1: Setting Up Apache Tomcat

1. **Download Tomcat**: Download the latest version of Apache Tomcat from the official website.

2. **Set Up in Your IDE**: If using an IDE like **IntelliJ IDEA** or **Eclipse**, integrate Tomcat by setting up a Tomcat server within the IDE's configuration.

3. **Create a Web Project**: In your IDE, create a new **Dynamic Web Project** (for example, in Eclipse or IntelliJ).

Step 2: Creating a Servlet

A Servlet handles HTTP requests sent by the client (browser) and generates HTTP responses.

- **Servlet Example**: Create a Java class that extends HttpServlet and overrides the doGet() or doPost() methods to handle HTTP requests.

```java
import javax.servlet.*;
import javax.servlet.http.*;
import java.io.*;

public class HelloServlet extends HttpServlet {
    @Override
    protected void doGet(HttpServletRequest request, HttpServletResponse response) throws ServletException, IOException {

        response.setContentType("text/html");
```

173

```
        PrintWriter        out        =
response.getWriter();
        out.println("<html><body>");
        out.println("<h1>Hello, World from
Servlet!</h1>");
        out.println("</body></html>");
    }
}
```

o This `HelloServlet` class handles GET requests and responds with an HTML message. When a user accesses the servlet, it generates an HTML page saying "Hello, World from Servlet!".

Step 3: Configuring the Web Deployment Descriptor (web.xml)

The `web.xml` file is used to configure the servlet mapping and other settings for your web application.

- **web.xml Example**:

xml

```
<?xml version="1.0" encoding="UTF-8"?>
<web-app
xmlns="http://java.sun.com/xml/ns/javaee"
xmlns:xsi="http://www.w3.org/2001/XMLSche
ma-instance"
xsi:schemaLocation="http://java.sun.com/x
```

```
ml/ns/javaee
http://java.sun.com/xml/ns/javaee/web-
app_3_0.xsd" version="3.0">
    <servlet>
        <servlet-
name>HelloServlet</servlet-name>
        <servlet-
class>HelloServlet</servlet-class>
    </servlet>
    <servlet-mapping>
        <servlet-
name>HelloServlet</servlet-name>
        <url-pattern>/hello</url-pattern>
    </servlet-mapping>
</web-app>
```

- o This configuration maps the `HelloServlet` to the URL pattern `/hello`. When users navigate to `http://localhost:8080/your-app-name/hello`, the `HelloServlet` will handle the request and generate a response.

Step 4: Creating a JSP

A **JavaServer Page (JSP)** is a simpler way to create dynamic web content. You can embed Java code into an HTML page, and it is compiled into a Servlet by the server.

- **JSP Example**:

175

```
jsp

<html>
<body>
    <h1>Hello from JSP!</h1>
    <p>The   current   time   is:   <%=   new
java.util.Date() %></p>
</body>
</html>
```

- o This JSP page will display "Hello from JSP!" along with the current date and time whenever it is accessed.

Step 5: Running the Application

- Deploy the project to the Tomcat server.
- Access the servlet through the URL: http://localhost:8080/your-app-name/hello.
- Access the JSP through the URL: http://localhost:8080/your-app-name/your-jsp-page.jsp.

Overview of Web Frameworks (Spring, JSF, Struts)

Java offers several web frameworks to simplify and structure web application development. Some of the most popular frameworks include:

- **Spring Framework**: The **Spring Framework** is the most widely used Java-based framework for building web applications. It provides comprehensive infrastructure support, including dependency injection (DI), aspect-oriented programming (AOP), and a variety of modules, including **Spring MVC** for building web applications.
    - ○ **Spring MVC**: A part of the Spring Framework, Spring MVC is a request-driven framework that follows the **Model-View-Controller** design pattern. It allows you to separate the different concerns of an application (model, view, and controller).
- **JSF (JavaServer Faces)**: **JSF** is a Java web framework for building user interfaces for web applications. It simplifies the development of Java-based web applications by providing a set of reusable UI components and the capability to handle events and state management.
- **Struts**: **Struts** is an older framework that was one of the first to implement the MVC design pattern. Although not as widely used today as Spring MVC, Struts is still a valuable framework for certain legacy systems.

177

Real-World Example: Developing a Simple Web-Based Task Manager

Now, let's apply everything we've learned to build a simple **task manager** web application using **Servlets** and **JSP**.

- **Step 1: Create a Task Model**: Create a simple `Task` class with attributes such as `id`, `title`, and `description`.

  java

```java
public class Task {
    private int id;
    private String title;
    private String description;

    public Task(int id, String title,
String description) {
        this.id = id;
        this.title = title;
        this.description = description;
    }

    public int getId() {
        return id;
    }
}
```

178

```
public String getTitle() {
    return title;
}

public String getDescription() {
    return description;
}
}
```

- **Step 2: Create a TaskServlet to Handle Requests**: This servlet will handle requests to create new tasks and list existing tasks.

```java
import javax.servlet.*;
import javax.servlet.http.*;
import java.io.*;
import java.util.*;

public class TaskServlet extends HttpServlet {
    private List<Task> taskList = new ArrayList<>();

    @Override
    protected void doGet(HttpServletRequest request,
```

179

```java
HttpServletResponse      response)      throws
ServletException, IOException {
        String          action          =
request.getParameter("action");

        if ("list".equals(action)) {
                request.setAttribute("tasks",
taskList);
                RequestDispatcher dispatcher =
request.getRequestDispatcher("taskList.js
p");
                dispatcher.forward(request,
response);
        }
    }


    @Override
    protected                           void
doPost(HttpServletRequest                request,
HttpServletResponse      response)      throws
ServletException, IOException {
        String          title           =
request.getParameter("title");
        String          description     =
request.getParameter("description");
        int id = taskList.size() + 1;

        Task newTask = new Task(id, title,
description);
```

180

```
        taskList.add(newTask);


response.sendRedirect("task?action=list")
;
    }
}
```

- **Step 3: Create the Task List JSP (taskList.jsp)**: This JSP page will display the list of tasks.

```jsp
<html>
<body>
    <h2>Task Manager</h2>
    <form action="task" method="POST">
        <label for="title">Title:</label>
        <input   type="text"   id="title"
name="title" required>
        <label
for="description">Description:</label>
        <input                type="text"
id="description"      name="description"
required>
        <input  type="submit"  value="Add
Task">
    </form>
    <h3>Task List</h3>
    <table border="1">
```

181

```
<tr>
    <th>ID</th>
    <th>Title</th>
    <th>Description</th>
</tr>
<c:forEach                var="task"
items="${tasks}">
    <tr>
        <td>${task.id}</td>
        <td>${task.title}</td>

<td>${task.description}</td>
    </tr>
</c:forEach>
</table>
</body>
</html>
```

- o In this JSP, we use **JSTL (JavaServer Pages Standard Tag Library)** tags to iterate over the list of tasks and display them in an HTML table.
- **Step 4: Configure web.xml for Servlet Mapping**: Finally, map the TaskServlet to a URL pattern in the web.xml deployment descriptor.

```
xml


<web-app
xmlns="http://java.sun.com/xml/ns/javaee"
```

182

```
xmlns:xsi="http://www.w3.org/2001/XMLSche
ma-instance"
xsi:schemaLocation="http://java.sun.com/x
ml/ns/javaee
http://java.sun.com/xml/ns/javaee/web-
app_3_0.xsd" version="3.0">
    <servlet>
        <servlet-
name>TaskServlet</servlet-name>
        <servlet-
class>TaskServlet</servlet-class>
    </servlet>
    <servlet-mapping>
        <servlet-
name>TaskServlet</servlet-name>
        <url-pattern>/task</url-pattern>
    </servlet-mapping>
</web-app>
```

Conclusion

This chapter provided an introduction to **Java Web Technologies** and guided you through setting up a simple **web application** using **Servlets** and **JSP**. We explored the basics of Java web development, including the setup of a servlet container (Tomcat) and the configuration of web applications using web.xml. We also discussed popular web frameworks like **Spring**, **JSF**, and **Struts**, and demonstrated how to build a **task manager** application that utilizes these technologies. In the next chapter, we will dive into **security** in Java web applications and best practices for securing sensitive data and preventing common vulnerabilities.

CHAPTER 14

SPRING FRAMEWORK BASICS

The **Spring Framework** is one of the most widely used Java frameworks for building enterprise-level applications. It simplifies Java development by providing comprehensive infrastructure support for developing Java applications. The framework focuses on improving modularity and making application development easier, particularly in the areas of dependency management, web development, and integration. This chapter will introduce the basics of the Spring Framework, explore **Dependency Injection** and **Inversion of Control (IoC)**, and explain how **Spring Boot** simplifies application development. Finally, we will build a **RESTful web service** using Spring Boot to demonstrate these concepts.

Introduction to the Spring Framework

The **Spring Framework** is an open-source framework that provides comprehensive programming and configuration support for Java applications. It is designed to simplify enterprise application development and to facilitate easier integration with third-party libraries and frameworks.

Some key features of Spring include:

- **Modularity**: Spring allows you to use only the modules you need, making it highly flexible and efficient.

- **Dependency Injection**: Spring provides a mechanism to inject dependencies into objects at runtime, making it easier to manage application components.

- **Aspect-Oriented Programming (AOP)**: Spring supports AOP, which allows you to separate cross-cutting concerns (like logging, transaction management, etc.) from your business logic.

- **Spring MVC**: A robust web framework that helps in building scalable web applications using the Model-View-Controller design pattern.

- **Integration**: Spring integrates seamlessly with various other technologies like Hibernate, JPA, JMS, and more.

Dependency Injection and Inversion of Control (IoC)

Dependency Injection (DI) and **Inversion of Control (IoC)** are central concepts in Spring. These two principles form the foundation for Spring's flexibility and modularity.

- **Inversion of Control (IoC)**: IoC is a design principle where the control of object creation and dependency management is shifted from the developer to a container or framework. In a traditional application, objects create their dependencies, but with IoC, the container creates and manages them. The Spring container is responsible for creating objects, managing their lifecycle, and injecting their dependencies.

- **Dependency Injection (DI)**: DI is a pattern where objects receive their dependencies (other objects they rely on) from an external source, rather than creating them internally. In Spring, DI can be done through **constructor injection**, **setter injection**, or **field injection**.

  o **Constructor Injection**: The dependencies are provided through the constructor. This is the most preferred method of DI because it ensures that dependencies are immutable and guarantees that the object is always fully initialized.

```java
@Component
public class Car {
    private Engine engine;

    @Autowired      // Marks the
constructor for dependency injection
    public Car(Engine engine) {
        this.engine = engine;
    }
```

```
public void start() {
    engine.run();
}
}
```

o **Setter Injection**: The dependencies are provided through setter methods. This allows the object to be created first and the dependencies to be set later.

```java

@Component
public class Car {
    private Engine engine;

    @Autowired   // Marks the setter
for dependency injection
    public    void    setEngine(Engine
engine) {
        this.engine = engine;
    }

    public void start() {
        engine.run();
    }
}
```

o **Field Injection**: Spring injects dependencies directly into the fields. This is less recommended as it makes the object difficult to test and harder to understand.

java

```
@Component
public class Car {
    @Autowired   // Marks the field
for dependency injection
    private Engine engine;

    public void start() {
        engine.run();
    }
}
```

• **Spring Container**: The Spring container is responsible for managing the objects and their dependencies. The container is typically configured using XML or annotations. The most common type of container is the **ApplicationContext**.

o **Example (Using ApplicationContext)**:

java

```
ApplicationContext    context   =   new
AnnotationConfigApplicationContext(
AppConfig.class);
Car              car            =
context.getBean(Car.class);
car.start();
```

Spring Boot for Simplified Application Development

Spring Boot is a tool that simplifies the process of setting up and configuring Spring-based applications. It removes the need for complex XML configuration and provides sensible defaults for common application setups. Spring Boot is designed to get you up and running quickly with minimal setup.

Key features of Spring Boot include:

- **Auto Configuration**: Automatically configures beans based on your application's requirements.
- **Embedded Web Server**: Includes built-in support for Tomcat, Jetty, and Undertow, so you don't need to deploy your application to a separate web server.
- **Spring Boot Starter Projects**: A collection of pre-configured dependencies for common use cases, such as web development, data access, security, etc.
- **Spring Boot Actuator**: Provides production-ready features like health checks, metrics, and monitoring.

- **Creating a Spring Boot Application**:
    1. Use the Spring Initializr (https://start.spring.io/) to generate a Spring Boot project.
    2. Select dependencies like **Spring Web**, **Spring Data JPA**, **Spring Boot DevTools**, etc.
    3. Create your main application class to run the Spring Boot application.
    ○ **Example of a Spring Boot Application**:

```java

import org.springframework.boot.SpringApplication;
import org.springframework.boot.autoconfigure.SpringBootApplication;

@SpringBootApplication  // Marks the class as a Spring Boot application
public class Application {
    public static void main(String[] args) {

SpringApplication.run(Application.class, args);
    }
}
```

- **Spring Boot Configuration**: Spring Boot uses **application.properties** or **application.yml** for external configuration (e.g., database connections, server ports).
  - **Example (application.properties)**:

```properties
server.port=8081
spring.datasource.url=jdbc:mysql://
localhost:3306/mydatabase
spring.datasource.username=root
spring.datasource.password=password
```

Real-World Example: Building a RESTful Web Service with Spring Boot

Let's build a simple **RESTful Web Service** using **Spring Boot**. This web service will allow users to create, read, update, and delete tasks (CRUD operations).

- **Step 1: Define a Task Model**:

```java
public class Task {
    private int id;
    private String description;
    private boolean completed;
```

```java
    // Getters and setters
    public int getId() {
        return id;
    }

    public void setId(int id) {
        this.id = id;
    }

    public String getDescription() {
        return description;
    }

    public void setDescription(String
description) {
        this.description = description;
    }

    public boolean isCompleted() {
        return completed;
    }

    public void setCompleted(boolean
completed) {
        this.completed = completed;
    }
}
```

193

- **Step 2: Create a Task Controller (REST API)**: Spring Boot provides **@RestController** to create REST APIs.

```java
import org.springframework.web.bind.annotation.*;
import java.util.ArrayList;
import java.util.List;

@RestController
@RequestMapping("/tasks")
public class TaskController {

    private List<Task> tasks = new ArrayList<>();

    // Get all tasks
    @GetMapping
    public List<Task> getTasks() {
        return tasks;
    }

    // Create a new task
    @PostMapping
    public Task createTask(@RequestBody Task task) {
        tasks.add(task);
```

194

```java
        return task;
    }


    // Update a task
    @PutMapping("/{id}")
    public Task updateTask(@PathVariable
int id, @RequestBody Task updatedTask) {
        Task          task          =
tasks.stream().filter(t -> t.getId() ==
id).findFirst().orElse(null);
        if (task != null) {

task.setDescription(updatedTask.getDescri
ption());

task.setCompleted(updatedTask.isCompleted
());
        }
        return task;
    }


    // Delete a task
    @DeleteMapping("/{id}")
    public void deleteTask(@PathVariable
int id) {
        tasks.removeIf(task           ->
task.getId() == id);
    }
}
```

- o **@GetMapping**: Handles HTTP GET requests to fetch all tasks.
- o **@PostMapping**: Handles HTTP POST requests to create a new task.
- o **@PutMapping**: Handles HTTP PUT requests to update a task.
- o **@DeleteMapping**: Handles HTTP DELETE requests to remove a task.

- **Step 3: Running the Spring Boot Application**: The application can be run with the following command:

```bash
bash
```

```
mvn spring-boot:run
```

Alternatively, you can run it directly from your IDE by running the `main` method of the `Application` class.

- **Step 4: Testing the REST API**: You can test the API using **Postman** or **curl**:
  - o **GET**: `http://localhost:8080/tasks`
  - o **POST**: `http://localhost:8080/tasks` with a JSON body like:

```json
json
```

```
{
    "id": 1,
```

```
        "description":   "Finish   Spring
    Boot tutorial",
        "completed": false
    }
```

- o **PUT**:   http://localhost:8080/tasks/1
  with a JSON body to update a task.
- o **DELETE**:
  http://localhost:8080/tasks/1 to delete
  a task.

Conclusion

This chapter introduced the **Spring Framework**, covering its core concepts like **Dependency Injection** and **Inversion of Control**. We also explored **Spring Boot**, which simplifies application development with sensible defaults and automatic configuration. By building a **RESTful web service** with Spring Boot, we demonstrated how easy it is to create robust web applications using Spring technologies. In the next chapter, we will dive into **Spring Security** to learn how to secure web applications and protect sensitive data.

CHAPTER 15

ADVANCED SPRING FRAMEWORK

In this chapter, we will explore advanced features of the **Spring Framework**, including **Aspect-Oriented Programming (AOP)**, **Spring Security** for authentication and authorization, and integrating **Spring Data** with **Hibernate** for ORM (Object-Relational Mapping). Additionally, we will demonstrate how to secure a REST API with authentication to showcase the power and flexibility of Spring in real-world applications.

Spring AOP (Aspect-Oriented Programming)

Aspect-Oriented Programming (AOP) is a programming paradigm that allows you to separate cross-cutting concerns, such as logging, transaction management, or security, from the business logic. In AOP, concerns like these are defined in separate modules called **aspects**. Spring AOP provides the tools to integrate AOP into your application.

- **Key Concepts of AOP**:
    - **Aspect**: A module that encapsulates cross-cutting concerns (e.g., logging, security).

198

o **Joinpoint**: A point in the execution of a program, such as a method call or object creation, where an aspect can be applied.

o **Advice**: Code that runs at a specific joinpoint, like before or after a method execution.

o **Pointcut**: A set of criteria that determine where advice should be applied.

o **Weaving**: The process of applying aspects to the target objects at runtime.

Spring AOP is typically used for method execution interception.

Example of AOP in Spring:

1. **Step 1: Define the Aspect**: You can define an aspect using @Aspect annotation and create an advice method with @Before, @After, @Around annotations.

```java
import org.aspectj.lang.annotation.Aspect;
import org.aspectj.lang.annotation.Before;
import org.springframework.stereotype.Component;

@Aspect
@Component
public class LoggingAspect {
```

```
@Before("execution(*
com.example.service.*.*(..))")
    public void logBefore() {
        System.out.println("Executing
method...");
    }
}
```

- o The above aspect will log a message before any method in the `com.example.service` package is executed.

2. **Step 2: Enable AOP in Spring Configuration**: You need to enable AOP support in your Spring configuration.

```java
import
org.springframework.context.annotation.Bean;
import
org.springframework.context.annotation.Configuration;
import
org.springframework.context.annotation.EnableAspectJAutoProxy;

@Configuration
@EnableAspectJAutoProxy
```

```
public class AppConfig {
    @Bean
    public LoggingAspect loggingAspect() {
        return new LoggingAspect();
    }
}
```

3. **Step 3: Using AOP**: When you run the application, the aspect will automatically intercept method executions in the specified package (`com.example.service`), and the advice will be triggered.

Spring Security and Authentication

Spring Security is a powerful and customizable authentication and access-control framework for Java applications. It is widely used for securing web applications by providing features like authentication, authorization, and protection against common attacks such as CSRF (Cross-Site Request Forgery).

- **Authentication**: Verifying the identity of a user, typically done with a username and password.
- **Authorization**: Determining whether the authenticated user has the necessary permissions to access a resource.

Basic Setup of Spring Security:

1. **Step 1: Add Dependencies**: To use Spring Security, add the following dependency in your `pom.xml` if you are using Maven:

xml

```
<dependency>

<groupId>org.springframework.boot</groupId>
    <artifactId>spring-boot-starter-security</artifactId>
</dependency>
```

2. **Step 2: Configure Web Security**: You can customize Spring Security by extending `WebSecurityConfigurerAdapter` and overriding the `configure` methods.

java

```
import org.springframework.context.annotation.Configuration;
import org.springframework.security.config.annotation.web.builders.HttpSecurity;
```

```java
import
org.springframework.security.config.annot
ation.web.configuration.EnableWebSecurity
;
import
org.springframework.security.config.annot
ation.web.configuration.WebSecurityConfig
urerAdapter;

@Configuration
@EnableWebSecurity
public class WebSecurityConfig extends
WebSecurityConfigurerAdapter {

    @Override
    protected void configure(HttpSecurity
http) throws Exception {
        http
            .authorizeRequests()

.antMatchers("/public/**").permitAll()  //
Allow public access
            .anyRequest().authenticated()
// Secure other endpoints
            .and()
            .formLogin().permitAll()    //
Enable form-based login
            .and()
```

203

```
            .logout().permitAll();        //
Enable logout
        }
    }
```

3. **Step 3: Customize Authentication**: To authenticate users, Spring Security supports various methods, including in-memory authentication, JDBC authentication, and custom authentication providers.

java

```
import
org.springframework.context.annotation.Be
an;
import
org.springframework.context.annotation.Co
nfiguration;
import
org.springframework.security.config.annot
ation.web.builders.HttpSecurity;
import
org.springframework.security.config.annot
ation.web.configuration.EnableWebSecurity
;
import
org.springframework.security.config.annot
ation.web.configuration.WebSecurityConfig
urerAdapter;
```

```java
import
org.springframework.security.core.userdet
ails.User;
import
org.springframework.security.core.userdet
ails.UserDetailsService;
import
org.springframework.security.core.userdet
ails.InMemoryUserDetailsManager;

@Configuration
@EnableWebSecurity
public class WebSecurityConfig extends
WebSecurityConfigurerAdapter {

    @Override
    protected void configure(HttpSecurity
http) throws Exception {
        http
            .authorizeRequests()

.antMatchers("/public/**").permitAll()
            .anyRequest().authenticated()
            .and()
            .formLogin().permitAll()
            .and()
            .logout().permitAll();
    }
```

```
@Bean
public            UserDetailsService
userDetailsService() {
    InMemoryUserDetailsManager manager
= new InMemoryUserDetailsManager();

manager.createUser(User.withUsername("use
r").password("{noop}password").roles("USE
R").build());
    return manager;
    }
}
```

- o In this example, we create an in-memory user with the username `user` and password `password` and assign the role `USER`.

4. **Step 4: Access-Control**: Spring Security allows you to define access control based on user roles. In the configuration above, we ensure that any request other than `/public/**` is authenticated.

Spring Data and Hibernate Integration

Spring Data simplifies database access by providing abstraction over traditional data access layers, such as **JDBC** or **JPA (Java Persistence API)**. **Hibernate** is the most popular implementation of JPA, and Spring integrates seamlessly with Hibernate to manage persistence.

- **Spring Data JPA**: Spring Data JPA reduces boilerplate code required to access data in relational databases by providing the JpaRepository interface. This interface includes common CRUD operations and custom queries, saving time and effort.

Example of Spring Data and Hibernate Integration:

1. **Step 1: Add Dependencies**: In your pom.xml, add dependencies for Spring Data JPA and Hibernate.

xml

```xml
<dependency>

<groupId>org.springframework.boot</groupId>
    <artifactId>spring-boot-starter-data-jpa</artifactId>
</dependency>
<dependency>
    <groupId>org.hibernate</groupId>
    <artifactId>hibernate-core</artifactId>
</dependency>
```

2. **Step 2: Define the Entity**: Create an entity class that will be mapped to the database table using Hibernate.

java

```java
import javax.persistence.Entity;
import javax.persistence.Id;

@Entity
public class Task {
    @Id
    private Long id;
    private String description;
    private boolean completed;

    // Getters and setters
}
```

3. **Step 3: Create a Repository**: Define a repository interface that extends `JpaRepository` to access `Task` entities.

java

```java
import
org.springframework.data.jpa.repository.J
paRepository;
```

```
public interface TaskRepository extends
JpaRepository<Task, Long> {
    // Custom query methods can be added
here
}
```

4. **Step 4: Use the Repository in a Service**: Inject the repository into a service class and use it to interact with the database.

```java
import
org.springframework.beans.factory.annotat
ion.Autowired;
import
org.springframework.stereotype.Service;

@Service
public class TaskService {

    @Autowired
    private TaskRepository taskRepository;

    public void addTask(Task task) {
        taskRepository.save(task);
    }

    public List<Task> getAllTasks() {
```

```
                    return taskRepository.findAll();
        }

    }
```

Real-World Example: Secure REST API with Authentication

Now, let's combine Spring Security and Spring Data to build a **secure REST API** for managing tasks. We'll use JWT (JSON Web Token) for authentication to ensure that only authenticated users can access the task management functionality.

1. **Step 1: Add JWT Dependencies**: Add the required dependencies for JWT and Spring Security.

   xml

   ```xml
   <dependency>
       <groupId>io.jsonwebtoken</groupId>
       <artifactId>jjwt</artifactId>
       <version>0.11.5</version>
   </dependency>
   ```

2. **Step 2: Create a TaskController**: Define a controller that exposes RESTful endpoints for managing tasks.

   java

```java
import
org.springframework.web.bind.annotation.*
;

@RestController
@RequestMapping("/api/tasks")
public class TaskController {

    @Autowired
    private TaskService taskService;

    @GetMapping
    public List<Task> getTasks() {
        return taskService.getAllTasks();
    }

    @PostMapping
    public Task createTask(@RequestBody
Task task) {
        taskService.addTask(task);
        return task;
    }
}
```

3. **Step 3: Implement JWT Authentication**: Use Spring Security to secure the API and implement JWT-based authentication.

```java
java
```

```
@Configuration
@EnableWebSecurity
public class WebSecurityConfig extends
WebSecurityConfigurerAdapter {

    @Override
    protected void configure(HttpSecurity
http) throws Exception {
        http
            .authorizeRequests()

.antMatchers("/api/authenticate").permitA
ll()
            .anyRequest().authenticated()
            .and()
            .httpBasic()
            .and()
            .csrf().disable();
    }
}
```

This configuration ensures that the
/api/authenticate endpoint is public, but all other
API endpoints are secured and require authentication.

Conclusion

This chapter covered advanced features of the **Spring Framework**, including **AOP**, **Spring Security**, and **Spring Data JPA** with **Hibernate** integration. We explored how to use AOP for handling cross-cutting concerns, implement secure authentication in REST APIs with Spring Security, and integrate Spring Data and Hibernate for seamless database management. The real-world example of securing a REST API with JWT authentication provided a practical demonstration of securing modern web applications using Spring technologies. In the next chapter, we will explore **Spring Boot advanced features** and dive deeper into microservices architecture.

CHAPTER 16

JAVAFX FOR BUILDING DESKTOP APPLICATIONS

In this chapter, we will explore **JavaFX**, a powerful framework for building **desktop applications** in Java. JavaFX provides a rich set of UI components, layouts, and event handling capabilities that allow you to create modern, interactive graphical user interfaces (GUIs). We'll cover the basics of JavaFX, including UI components, layouts, and event handling. We'll also walk through building a **simple personal finance manager** as a real-world example of a desktop application.

Introduction to JavaFX and UI Components

JavaFX is a platform for building and deploying rich client applications that operate on desktops, embedded systems, and mobile devices. It includes a set of graphics and media packages to enable developers to design visually appealing user interfaces.

Some key features of JavaFX include:

- **FXML**: An XML-based language used to define the structure of the UI.

- **Scene Graph**: The tree structure that holds all the visual elements in a JavaFX application.
- **CSS**: JavaFX supports **Cascading Style Sheets** for styling the UI components, similar to web development.
- **Rich Media Support**: JavaFX supports audio, video, and image formats for building multimedia-rich applications.

JavaFX includes a variety of **UI components** for building interactive interfaces:

- **Labels**: Displays text in a UI.
- **Buttons**: Triggers actions when clicked.
- **TextFields**: Allows users to input text.
- **ComboBoxes**: Provides a dropdown list of options.
- **Tables**: Displays data in tabular form.

Layouts, Controls, and Event Handling in JavaFX

JavaFX provides a set of **layout containers** that help organize the UI components in an application. Layouts define how child elements are arranged within their parent containers.

Common Layouts in JavaFX:

1. **BorderPane**: Divides the screen into five regions—top, bottom, left, right, and center.

2. **GridPane**: Organizes the content into a flexible grid of rows and columns.

3. **VBox and HBox**: Vertical and horizontal box layouts that arrange elements in a single column or row.

4. **FlowPane**: Arranges components in a flow that wraps when necessary.

Basic UI Controls:

JavaFX provides a variety of **controls** to interact with users:

- **TextField**: A single-line text input field.
- **Button**: A clickable button.
- **CheckBox**: A box that can be checked or unchecked.
- **ComboBox**: A dropdown list to select from predefined options.

Event Handling:

In JavaFX, event handling involves registering event handlers to UI components. The most common events are:

- **Mouse Events**: For detecting clicks, mouse movements, etc.
- **Keyboard Events**: For detecting key presses and releases.

Example of event handling for a button click:

```java
java
```

```java
Button button = new Button("Click Me");
button.setOnAction(e -> {
    System.out.println("Button clicked!");
});
```

This lambda expression sets an event handler to print a message when the button is clicked.

Building Desktop Applications with JavaFX

Building desktop applications with JavaFX involves the following steps:

1. **Create a Stage**: The main window of your application.
2. **Create a Scene**: The content that will be displayed in the window.
3. **Add UI Components**: Use controls, layouts, and other components to build the UI.
4. **Event Handling**: Set up event handlers to make the UI interactive.
5. **Start the Application**: Launch the application by creating an instance of the JavaFX application class.

Basic JavaFX Application Structure:

```java
java
```

```java
import javafx.application.Application;
import javafx.scene.Scene;
import javafx.scene.control.Button;
import javafx.scene.layout.StackPane;
import javafx.stage.Stage;

public class MyJavaFXApp extends Application {

    @Override
    public void start(Stage primaryStage) {
        Button btn = new Button("Click Me");
        btn.setOnAction(e                      ->
System.out.println("Button clicked!"));

        StackPane root = new StackPane();
        root.getChildren().add(btn);

        Scene scene = new Scene(root, 300, 250);
        primaryStage.setTitle("JavaFX
Application");
        primaryStage.setScene(scene);
        primaryStage.show();
    }

    public static void main(String[] args) {
        launch(args);
    }
}
```

- **Application Class**: This is the main class for JavaFX applications, and it extends `Application`. The `start()` method is overridden to set up the UI.
- **Stage**: Represents the window.
- **Scene**: Contains all the visual elements.
- **StackPane**: A layout pane that arranges components in a stack.

Real-World Example: Developing a Simple Personal Finance Manager

Let's build a **Personal Finance Manager** desktop application using JavaFX. This application will allow users to:

1. Add income or expense entries.
2. Display a list of transactions.
3. Calculate the balance (income minus expenses).

Step 1: Define the Transaction Model:

We will create a `Transaction` class to hold information about each transaction (amount and type).

java

```
public class Transaction {
    private String type;
```

```java
    private double amount;

    public    Transaction(String    type,    double
amount) {
        this.type = type;
        this.amount = amount;
    }

    public String getType() {
        return type;
    }

    public double getAmount() {
        return amount;
    }

    @Override
    public String toString() {
        return type + ": " + amount;
    }
}
```

Step 2: Create the User Interface:

The UI will allow the user to input the transaction type (income or expense), the amount, and display a list of transactions.

```java
java

import javafx.application.Application;
```

```java
import javafx.beans.value.ChangeListener;
import javafx.beans.value.ObservableValue;
import javafx.scene.Scene;
import javafx.scene.control.*;
import javafx.scene.layout.VBox;
import javafx.stage.Stage;

import java.util.ArrayList;
import java.util.List;

public class FinanceManagerApp extends Application {

    private List<Transaction> transactions = new ArrayList<>();
    private ListView<String> transactionList = new ListView<>();
    private TextField amountField = new TextField();
    private ComboBox<String> typeComboBox = new ComboBox<>();
    private Label balanceLabel = new Label("Balance: $0.0");

    @Override
    public void start(Stage primaryStage) {
        // Set up transaction type options
```

```java
typeComboBox.getItems().addAll("Income",
"Expense");

typeComboBox.getSelectionModel().selectFirst();

        // Set up transaction button
        Button    addButton   =   new    Button("Add
Transaction");
        addButton.setOnAction(e                -> 
addTransaction());

        // Set up layout
        VBox layout = new VBox(10);
        layout.getChildren().addAll(
                new Label("Transaction Type:"),
typeComboBox,
                new           Label("Amount:"),
amountField,
                addButton,                     new 
Label("Transactions:"),        transactionList,
balanceLabel
        );

        // Set up the scene and stage
        Scene  scene  =  new  Scene(layout,  300,
400);
        primaryStage.setTitle("Personal   Finance
Manager");
```

```
        primaryStage.setScene(scene);
        primaryStage.show();
    }


    // Add a transaction to the list
    private void addTransaction() {
        try {
            double          amount          =
Double.parseDouble(amountField.getText());
            String          type            =
typeComboBox.getValue();

            Transaction  transaction  =  new
Transaction(type, amount);
            transactions.add(transaction);

            // Update UI components

transactionList.getItems().add(transaction.toSt
ring());
            updateBalance();
        } catch (NumberFormatException e) {
            showErrorDialog("Please   enter   a
valid amount.");
        }
    }

    // Update balance label
    private void updateBalance() {
```

```java
        double balance = 0.0;
        for    (Transaction    transaction    :
transactions) {
            if
(transaction.getType().equals("Income")) {
                balance                      +=
transaction.getAmount();
            } else {
                balance                      -=
transaction.getAmount();
            }
        }
        balanceLabel.setText("Balance:    $"    +
balance);
    }


    // Show error message
    private void showErrorDialog(String message)
{
        Alert        alert        =        new
Alert(Alert.AlertType.ERROR);
        alert.setTitle("Error");
        alert.setHeaderText(null);
        alert.setContentText(message);
        alert.showAndWait();
    }

    public static void main(String[] args) {
        launch(args);
```

```
    }
}
```

Explanation of the Application:

1. **UI Components**:
   - **ComboBox**: Used for selecting the transaction type (income or expense).
   - **TextField**: Used for entering the transaction amount.
   - **ListView**: Displays the list of transactions.
   - **Label**: Displays the current balance of the user.
2. **Transaction Logic**:
   - The `addTransaction` method adds the transaction to the list and updates the transaction list view.
   - The `updateBalance` method calculates the balance based on the list of transactions.
3. **Error Handling**:
   - An error dialog is shown if the user inputs an invalid amount (non-numeric value).

Conclusion

In this chapter, we explored **JavaFX** for building desktop applications, focusing on the core concepts of UI components, layouts, and event handling. We also created a **simple personal**

225

finance manager that allows users to add income or expense entries, display transactions, and calculate the balance. JavaFX provides a powerful toolset for building modern desktop applications, and understanding its core components is essential for developing interactive and user-friendly applications. In the next chapter, we will delve into **JavaFX advanced topics**, such as animations, effects, and data binding.

CHAPTER 17

TESTING JAVA APPLICATIONS

In this chapter, we will explore the critical aspect of **unit testing** in Java applications. Unit testing is essential for ensuring that individual components of your application work correctly and that changes made to the codebase do not introduce unexpected bugs. We will cover popular testing frameworks like **JUnit** and **TestNG**, introduce the concept of **mocking**, and discuss **Test-Driven Development (TDD)**. Finally, we will implement a real-world example of unit testing in an **e-commerce application** to demonstrate how testing can be integrated into the development process.

Importance of Unit Testing

Unit testing involves testing individual units or components of a software system in isolation to verify that they work as expected. The main benefits of unit testing include:

- **Ensuring Correctness**: Unit tests ensure that each method or function performs as intended and returns the correct output for various input cases.

- **Preventing Regression**: Unit tests help prevent previously fixed issues from reappearing when new features or fixes are added.

- **Facilitating Refactoring**: When you have a suite of unit tests, you can refactor your code with confidence, knowing that the tests will catch any unintended changes in behavior.

- **Improving Code Quality**: Writing tests encourages developers to think more deeply about edge cases and potential errors in their code, improving overall code quality.

Writing Unit Tests with JUnit and TestNG

There are several popular testing frameworks for Java, but **JUnit** and **TestNG** are the most commonly used. Both frameworks allow you to define test cases, set up test data, and assert that the expected results match the actual results.

JUnit Basics:

JUnit is a widely used testing framework in Java. It provides annotations to define test methods and lifecycle hooks to set up and tear down tests.

- **JUnit 5** introduces several new features, including the ability to run tests in parallel, advanced assertions, and parameterized tests.

- **Example (Basic Unit Test with JUnit 5)**:

```java
import org.junit.jupiter.api.Test;
import static org.junit.jupiter.api.Assertions.*;

public class CalculatorTest {

    @Test
    void testAddition() {
        Calculator calculator = new Calculator();
        int result = calculator.add(2, 3);
        assertEquals(5, result, "Addition should return correct result");
    }
}
```

- o **Annotations**:
  - @Test: Marks a method as a test method.
  - assertEquals(expected, actual): Asserts that the expected value equals the actual value.

TestNG Basics:

TestNG is another popular testing framework with more advanced features, including support for parameterized tests, grouping, and parallel test execution.

- **Example (Basic Unit Test with TestNG):**

```java
import org.testng.annotations.Test;
import static org.testng.Assert.*;

public class CalculatorTest {

    @Test
    public void testAddition() {
        Calculator calculator = new Calculator();
        int result = calculator.add(2, 3);
        assertEquals(result, 5, "Addition should return correct result");
    }
}
```

- o **Annotations:**
  - ▪ @Test: Marks a method as a test method.

- assertEquals(expected, actual): Asserts that the expected value equals the actual value.

Mocking and Test-Driven Development (TDD)

Mocking is a technique used in unit testing to simulate dependencies that a class or method relies on. It helps isolate the unit being tested by replacing real dependencies with mock objects, ensuring that tests are focused on the unit's behavior, not on external systems or complex interactions.

Mocking:

Mocking frameworks like **Mockito** and **EasyMock** allow you to create mock objects, specify their behavior, and verify interactions.

- **Mockito Example**: Mockito is a popular mocking framework for Java that allows you to mock objects and verify method calls.

```java
import static org.mockito.Mockito.*;
import org.junit.jupiter.api.Test;
```

231

```java
public class UserServiceTest {

    @Test
    void testGetUserDetails() {
        // Mocking the UserRepository
        UserRepository     mockRepo     =
mock(UserRepository.class);

when(mockRepo.getUserById(1)).thenReturn(
new User(1, "John Doe"));

        // Creating the service and passing
the mocked repository
        UserService   userService   =   new
UserService(mockRepo);

        // Running the test
        User             user             =
userService.getUserDetails(1);
        assertEquals("John          Doe",
user.getName());
    }
}
```

o In this example, we mock the UserRepository
   to return a User object when getUserById(1)
   is called. This allows us to test the UserService
   class without needing an actual database or data
   source.

232

Test-Driven Development (TDD):

Test-Driven Development is a software development approach where you write tests before writing the actual code. The process involves the following steps:

1. **Write a test** that defines the behavior of the function or method.
2. **Run the test** (which should fail initially because the code hasn't been written yet).
3. **Write the code** to make the test pass.
4. **Refactor** the code while ensuring the tests still pass.
5. **Repeat** the process for other functionalities.

TDD helps ensure that the code is thoroughly tested and often results in better-designed, more modular code.

Real-World Example: Unit Testing in an E-Commerce Application

In this example, we will demonstrate how unit testing can be applied in an **e-commerce application**. This application includes functionality for processing customer orders, calculating total prices, and applying discounts.

Step 1: Define the `OrderService`:

The `OrderService` class is responsible for calculating the total price of an order.

java

```java
public class OrderService {

    private DiscountService discountService;

    public          OrderService(DiscountService
discountService) {
        this.discountService = discountService;
    }

    public double calculateTotal(Order order) {
        double total = 0.0;
        for (Item item : order.getItems()) {
            total += item.getPrice();
        }
        total                                    =
discountService.applyDiscount(total);
        return total;
    }
}
```

Step 2: Define the `DiscountService`:

The `DiscountService` applies discounts to the total price.

234

```java

public class DiscountService {

    public double applyDiscount(double total) {
        if (total > 100) {
            return total * 0.9;  // 10% discount
for orders over $100
        }
        return total;
    }
}
```

Step 3: Create Unit Tests:

Now, let's write unit tests for the OrderService. We'll mock the DiscountService dependency and verify that the OrderService correctly calculates the total price.

```java

import org.junit.jupiter.api.Test;
import static org.mockito.Mockito.*;
import                                     static
org.junit.jupiter.api.Assertions.*;

public class OrderServiceTest {

    @Test
    void testCalculateTotalWithDiscount() {
```

```java
        // Arrange: Create a mock DiscountService
        DiscountService    discountService    =
mock(DiscountService.class);

when(discountService.applyDiscount(150.0)).then
Return(135.0); // Mock behavior

        // Arrange: Create an OrderService with
the mocked DiscountService
        OrderService    orderService    =    new
OrderService(discountService);

        // Create an order with 150 total price
        Order order = new Order();
        order.addItem(new Item("Laptop", 150));

        // Act: Calculate the total price
        double              total              =
orderService.calculateTotal(order);

        // Assert: Verify the total price after
applying discount
        assertEquals(135.0,   total,   "The   total
price should have a 10% discount applied.");
    }
}
```

- **Explanation**:

- o We mock the `DiscountService` and specify that when the total price is `150.0`, it should return `135.0` (applying a 10% discount).
- o We create an order with one item (`Laptop` costing $150), and call `orderService.calculateTotal()`.
- o The test verifies that the total price after the discount is applied is correct.

Conclusion

This chapter introduced the importance of **unit testing** in Java applications and provided an in-depth look at popular testing frameworks like **JUnit** and **TestNG**. We covered the concepts of **mocking** and **Test-Driven Development (TDD)**, which help ensure that applications are thoroughly tested and maintainable. By walking through the process of unit testing an **e-commerce application**, we demonstrated how to write and structure tests in a real-world scenario. In the next chapter, we will explore **integration testing** and **continuous integration (CI)** practices to ensure that different parts of your application work together correctly.

CHAPTER 18

DEPENDENCY MANAGEMENT WITH MAVEN AND GRADLE

In this chapter, we will explore the concept of **build automation** and **dependency management** in Java applications. **Maven** and **Gradle** are two of the most widely used tools for managing dependencies, automating builds, and simplifying the development process. We will introduce both tools, explain how they manage dependencies, and walk through a real-world example of setting up a project using **Maven**.

Understanding Build Automation Tools

Build automation is the process of automating the steps involved in compiling, testing, packaging, and deploying an application. These tools ensure that the build process is repeatable, consistent, and easy to manage, especially in large projects with many dependencies.

Build tools typically help with the following tasks:

1. **Compiling Code**: Converting source code (Java files) into bytecode (.class files).

2. **Dependency Management**: Handling external libraries (JARs) and ensuring that the right versions are used.

3. **Running Tests**: Running unit tests and generating test reports.

4. **Packaging**: Creating JAR/WAR/EAR files for deployment.

5. **Deployment**: Uploading artifacts to remote repositories or servers.

Both **Maven** and **Gradle** are powerful tools that automate these tasks and help developers maintain clean and efficient project structures.

Introduction to Maven and Gradle

- **Maven**: **Apache Maven** is a build automation tool primarily used for Java projects. Maven uses an XML configuration file (`pom.xml`) to define project structure, dependencies, plugins, and build instructions. It is widely used for dependency management and builds projects with a predefined lifecycle.
  - o **Key Features**:
    - **Dependency Management**: Maven uses a central repository to download dependencies (JAR files) and manage version conflicts.

- **Convention Over Configuration**: Maven follows standard conventions for project structure (e.g., `src/main/java` for source code).

- **Plugins**: A wide variety of plugins are available to perform tasks like compiling code, running tests, packaging, and deploying.

- **Gradle**: **Gradle** is a more flexible and powerful build tool that uses a **Groovy-based DSL** (domain-specific language) for configuration. Unlike Maven, which uses XML, Gradle uses a declarative approach with a `build.gradle` file, which is concise and easier to understand.

  o **Key Features**:

    - **Incremental Builds**: Gradle optimizes builds by tracking changes and only rebuilding the necessary parts of the project.

    - **Dependency Management**: Gradle can use Maven and Ivy repositories for dependency management.

    - **Groovy DSL**: Provides a more flexible and expressive way to define the build process.

- **Performance**: Gradle is known for its high performance, especially in large projects, due to features like caching and parallel execution.

Managing Dependencies and Build Lifecycle

Both **Maven** and **Gradle** provide mechanisms to manage dependencies, handle various build tasks, and define build lifecycles. Understanding these tools' mechanisms helps you automate and optimize your build process.

- **Maven Dependency Management**: Maven uses a `pom.xml` file (Project Object Model) to define the structure of the project, its dependencies, and other configurations. The dependencies are listed under the `<dependencies>` tag, and Maven will download the required libraries from central or private repositories.

  o **Example `pom.xml`:**

  ```
  xml
  ```

  ```
  <project
  xmlns="http://maven.apache.org/POM/
  4.0.0"
  ```

241

```
xmlns:xsi="http://www.w3.org/2001/X
MLSchema-instance"

xsi:schemaLocation="http://maven.ap
ache.org/POM/4.0.0
http://maven.apache.org/xsd/maven-
4.0.0.xsd">

<modelVersion>4.0.0</modelVersion>

    <groupId>com.example</groupId>

<artifactId>myproject</artifactId>
    <version>1.0-SNAPSHOT</version>

    <dependencies>
        <dependency>

<groupId>org.springframework</group
Id>
            <artifactId>spring-
core</artifactId>

<version>5.3.8</version>
        </dependency>
        <dependency>

<groupId>junit</groupId>
```

```
<artifactId>junit</artifactId>

<version>4.13.2</version>
        <scope>test</scope>
    </dependency>
  </dependencies>

</project>
```

- In this `pom.xml` example, two dependencies are specified: `spring-core` and `junit`. Maven will automatically fetch these libraries from the central repository.

- **Gradle Dependency Management**: Gradle uses the `build.gradle` file to declare dependencies. Gradle also supports **repositories** where dependencies are stored (like Maven Central or custom repositories).

  o **Example `build.gradle`**:

```gradle
gradle

plugins {
    id 'java'
}

repositories {
```

```
        mavenCentral()
}


dependencies {
    implementation
'org.springframework:spring-
core:5.3.8'
    testImplementation
'junit:junit:4.13.2'
}
```

- In this Gradle example, the dependencies are declared using `implementation` for production dependencies and `testImplementation` for test dependencies.

Real-World Example: Setting Up a Project with Maven

Now, let's walk through the process of setting up a simple **Java project using Maven**. This example will involve creating a project that uses **JUnit** for testing and **Spring Core** for a small application.

Step 1: Install Maven

1. **Download Maven**: Download Maven from the official site: https://maven.apache.org/download.cgi.
2. **Set Up Environment**: Set the `M2_HOME` environment variable and add Maven's `bin` directory to your system's `PATH`.

Step 2: Create a Maven Project

You can create a Maven project either manually or using an IDE like **IntelliJ IDEA** or **Eclipse**. For simplicity, let's manually create a project structure.

1. **Project Structure**:

    css

```
my-maven-project
├── pom.xml
└── src
    ├── main
    │   └── java
    │       └── com
    │           └── example
    │               └── App.java
    └── test
        └── java
            └── com
```

```
└── example
    └── AppTest.java
```

2. **pom.xml File**: Create the pom.xml file in the root of the project. This file contains the project configuration, dependencies, and build lifecycle.

xml

```xml
<project
xmlns="http://maven.apache.org/POM/4.0.0"

xmlns:xsi="http://www.w3.org/2001/XMLSche
ma-instance"

xsi:schemaLocation="http://maven.apache.o
rg/POM/4.0.0
http://maven.apache.org/xsd/maven-
4.0.0.xsd">
    <modelVersion>4.0.0</modelVersion>

    <groupId>com.example</groupId>
    <artifactId>my-maven-
project</artifactId>
    <version>1.0-SNAPSHOT</version>

    <dependencies>
        <!-- Spring Core -->
        <dependency>
```

```
<groupId>org.springframework</groupId>
        <artifactId>spring-
core</artifactId>
        <version>5.3.8</version>
    </dependency>

    <!-- JUnit for testing -->
    <dependency>
        <groupId>junit</groupId>

<artifactId>junit</artifactId>
        <version>4.13.2</version>
        <scope>test</scope>
    </dependency>
  </dependencies>
</project>
```

3. **App.java**: Create a simple Java class that we will test.

```java
package com.example;

public class App {
    public String greet(String name) {
        return "Hello, " + name;
    }
}
```

4. **AppTest.java**: Create a test class to test the greet()
   method.

```java
java

package com.example;

import org.junit.Test;
import                               static
org.junit.Assert.assertEquals;

public class AppTest {

    @Test
    public void testGreet() {
        App app = new App();
        String result = app.greet("John");
        assertEquals("Hello,          John",
result);
    }
}
```

Step 3: Build and Run the Project

1. **Compile the Project**: From the terminal, navigate to the
   project directory and run:

```bash
bash

mvn compile
```

2. **Run the Tests**: To run the tests using Maven:

```bash
mvn test
```

Maven will automatically download the dependencies (JUnit and Spring Core), compile the code, and execute the tests. If everything is set up correctly, Maven will show that the tests passed.

3. **Package the Application**: To package the application into a JAR file:

```bash
mvn package
```

The JAR file will be generated under the `target` directory.

Conclusion

In this chapter, we introduced **build automation tools** like **Maven** and **Gradle** that streamline the development process by automating tasks like compiling code, running tests, and managing dependencies. We explored the **dependency management** features of Maven and Gradle and walked through setting up a **Java project with Maven**. By the end of this chapter, you should have a solid understanding of how to use these tools to manage dependencies and automate your build process, improving the efficiency and consistency of your development workflow. In the next chapter, we will delve into **continuous integration (CI)** and **continuous delivery (CD)** practices for modern Java applications.

CHAPTER 19

JAVA FOR CLOUD DEVELOPMENT

In this chapter, we will explore **cloud computing** concepts and how Java can be leveraged to build, deploy, and scale applications in the cloud. We will cover cloud service models such as **IaaS (Infrastructure as a Service), PaaS (Platform as a Service)**, and **SaaS (Software as a Service)**, and discuss how Java applications can interact with popular cloud providers like **AWS (Amazon Web Services)**, **Microsoft Azure**, and **Google Cloud**. We will also walk through the process of **deploying Java applications** on the cloud with a real-world example of deploying a Java-based web application.

Cloud Concepts: IaaS, PaaS, and SaaS

Cloud computing offers a range of services that can be categorized into three primary service models: **IaaS**, **PaaS**, and **SaaS**. These models provide different levels of control, flexibility, and management responsibilities to both developers and businesses.

1. **Infrastructure as a Service (IaaS)**:

- o IaaS provides **virtualized computing resources** over the internet. It gives you full control over the infrastructure (like servers, storage, and networking) while abstracting away the physical hardware management.

- o **Examples**: AWS EC2, Google Compute Engine, Microsoft Azure Virtual Machines.

- o **Use Case**: You have control over the entire virtual machine and the operating system, and you need to manage the applications and software that run on it.

- o **IaaS in Java**: Java applications running on IaaS typically require you to manage the server and application runtime environment. For example, using **AWS EC2** to deploy and manage your Java-based application.

2. **Platform as a Service (PaaS)**:

- o PaaS provides a higher level of abstraction where the cloud provider manages the infrastructure, operating system, and runtime environment. You focus on developing the application, and the provider takes care of everything else.

- o **Examples**: AWS Elastic Beanstalk, Google App Engine, Microsoft Azure App Service.

- ○ **Use Case**: You want to focus on coding and application logic without worrying about managing the underlying infrastructure.
- ○ **PaaS in Java**: Java developers can deploy applications using platforms like **AWS Elastic Beanstalk** or **Google App Engine**. These platforms automatically manage the deployment, scaling, and monitoring of your Java application.

3. **Software as a Service (SaaS)**:
- ○ SaaS provides ready-to-use software applications over the internet. These applications are hosted and maintained by the provider and are accessed through a web interface.
- ○ **Examples**: Google Workspace, Microsoft 365, Salesforce.
- ○ **Use Case**: Users only need to interact with the application interface and are not concerned with the underlying code or infrastructure.
- ○ **SaaS in Java**: While Java applications aren't typically considered SaaS products, Java can be used to build SaaS applications that are hosted in the cloud. For example, building a customer relationship management (CRM) SaaS app with Java and deploying it to **Google Cloud** or **AWS**.

Using Java with Cloud Providers (AWS, Azure, Google Cloud)

Java is a widely supported language across all major cloud platforms, including **AWS**, **Microsoft Azure**, and **Google Cloud**. These platforms offer various services and tools to help developers build, deploy, and manage Java applications in the cloud.

1. **AWS (Amazon Web Services)**: AWS is one of the leading cloud providers, offering services like **Amazon EC2** (virtual servers), **Elastic Beanstalk** (PaaS for Java), **S3** (storage), and **RDS** (managed relational databases).

   o **Java SDK**: AWS provides an **AWS SDK for Java**, which includes libraries to interact with various AWS services (e.g., EC2, S3, DynamoDB, and more).

   o **Elastic Beanstalk for Java**: AWS Elastic Beanstalk simplifies Java application deployment by automatically handling the infrastructure and scaling.

   Example: Deploying a Java web application to AWS Elastic Beanstalk:

   o Create an AWS account and set up Elastic Beanstalk.

- o Package the Java web application as a WAR file (for a web app).
- o Deploy the WAR file to Elastic Beanstalk, which will automatically handle the deployment and scaling.

2. **Microsoft Azure**: Microsoft Azure is another popular cloud provider that offers a variety of services for Java developers, including **Azure App Service** (PaaS), **Azure Virtual Machines** (IaaS), and **Azure SQL Database** (managed database).

- o **Azure SDK for Java**: Azure provides an SDK for Java developers, including libraries for managing resources like virtual machines, databases, and storage accounts.
- o **Azure App Service for Java**: Azure App Service allows you to quickly deploy Java web applications without managing the infrastructure, similar to AWS Elastic Beanstalk.

Example: Deploying a Java web application to Azure App Service:

- o Create an Azure account and set up a new App Service.
- o Configure the app to use the Java runtime.
- o Deploy the WAR file or JAR file using Git or Azure DevOps for continuous deployment.

3. **Google Cloud**: Google Cloud offers services like **Google App Engine** (PaaS for Java), **Google Compute Engine** (IaaS), and **Cloud SQL** (managed database service).

   o **Google Cloud SDK for Java**: The SDK provides APIs for interacting with Google Cloud services like **Compute Engine**, **Cloud Storage**, and **BigQuery**.

   o **Google App Engine for Java**: Google App Engine provides a platform for deploying Java applications without worrying about the underlying infrastructure. It automatically scales applications based on demand.

Example: Deploying a Java web application to Google App Engine:

   o Install the **Google Cloud SDK**.
   o Create a new project on Google Cloud Console.
   o Package the Java web application (WAR or JAR) and deploy it to App Engine using the `goloud` command-line tool.

Deploying Java Applications on the Cloud

Deploying Java applications to the cloud involves several steps, depending on the cloud provider and the deployment model you choose (IaaS, PaaS, or SaaS). Here, we will focus on **deploying a Java web application** using a **PaaS solution**, as it is the most common approach for cloud-native Java applications.

Step 1: Preparing Your Java Application

Before deploying to the cloud, ensure that your Java application is ready:

1. **Build the Application**: Use tools like **Maven** or **Gradle** to build the project.
2. **Package the Application**: Package your application into a **JAR** (Java Application) or **WAR** (Web Application) file, depending on the deployment platform.
3. **Check Dependencies**: Make sure all external dependencies are included in the build file (e.g., `pom.xml` for Maven, `build.gradle` for Gradle).

Step 2: Deploying to Cloud Providers

Each cloud platform has a slightly different deployment process. Here's a general overview:

1. **AWS Elastic Beanstalk**:
   - Create an **Elastic Beanstalk** environment (e.g., Tomcat, Java SE).
   - Deploy the packaged WAR file using the **Elastic Beanstalk Console** or the AWS CLI.

o Elastic Beanstalk automatically sets up the required infrastructure (EC2 instances, load balancing, etc.).

2. **Microsoft Azure App Service**:

   o Create an **App Service** in the Azure Portal.

   o Configure the runtime stack to use Java (select the correct version).

   o Deploy the WAR file via Git, **Azure DevOps**, or directly from your local machine using **Git** or **FTP**.

3. **Google App Engine**:

   o Create a new **App Engine** project on **Google Cloud Console**.

   o Configure the `app.yaml` file (App Engine configuration file).

   o Deploy the application using the **gcloud CLI**:

   bash

```
gcloud app deploy
```

Real-World Example: Cloud Deployment of a Java-based Web Application

Let's walk through deploying a **simple Java web application** using **AWS Elastic Beanstalk**.

1. **Step 1: Set Up AWS Elastic Beanstalk**:

    o   Create an **AWS account** and navigate to **Elastic Beanstalk** in the AWS Console.

    o   Select **Create Application** and choose the **Java** platform.

    o   Select **Tomcat** or another Java runtime that matches your application's needs.

2. **Step 2: Prepare Your Java Application**:

    o   Ensure your Java web application is packaged as a **WAR file**.

    o   Use **Maven** to build the WAR file:

    ```bash
    mvn clean package
    ```

3. **Step 3: Deploy to Elastic Beanstalk**:

    o   Open the **Elastic Beanstalk Console**, select your application, and choose **Upload and Deploy**.

    o   Select your WAR file and deploy it.

4. **Step 4: Access Your Application**:

    o   After deployment, Elastic Beanstalk will provide a URL where your application is hosted. You can use this URL to access your Java web application.

Conclusion

In this chapter, we covered key concepts in **cloud development** and demonstrated how **Java** can be integrated with popular cloud providers like **AWS, Azure**, and **Google Cloud**. We discussed the different cloud service models (**IaaS, PaaS, SaaS**) and how they can be used to deploy Java applications. The real-world example of deploying a Java web application to **AWS Elastic Beanstalk** showed how easy it is to take advantage of cloud platforms for deploying and scaling Java applications. In the next chapter, we will explore **microservices architecture** and how Java can be used to build scalable, maintainable systems in the cloud.

CHAPTER 20

MICROSERVICES ARCHITECTURE WITH JAVA

In this chapter, we will dive into **microservices architecture** and explore how to design, build, and deploy microservices using **Java** and **Spring Boot**. Microservices architecture is an approach to software development where an application is structured as a collection of loosely coupled services. Each service is independently deployable, scalable, and focused on a specific business functionality. We will also cover key concepts such as **API Gateway**, **Service Discovery**, and demonstrate these concepts with a **real-world example** of a **microservice-based e-commerce system**.

Introduction to Microservices and Benefits

Microservices Architecture is an architectural style where an application is divided into a set of smaller, loosely coupled services, each of which implements a specific business function. Each microservice typically has its own database, is independently deployable, and communicates with other services via lightweight protocols (usually HTTP or messaging systems like Kafka).

Benefits of Microservices Architecture:

1. **Scalability**: Since each service is independent, you can scale the services that need more resources, rather than scaling the entire application.
2. **Flexibility**: Different services can be built using different technologies and programming languages (polyglot persistence and polyglot programming).
3. **Resilience**: Microservices are isolated, so a failure in one service does not impact the entire application.
4. **Faster Development**: Smaller teams can work on individual services, allowing for faster development cycles and continuous integration/continuous deployment (CI/CD).
5. **Easier Maintenance**: Each microservice can be independently updated and maintained, reducing the complexity of managing large monolithic codebases.

Challenges of Microservices:

- **Complexity**: Managing multiple services and their interactions can be complex, especially as the number of services grows.

- **Data Management**: Ensuring consistency across services and managing distributed databases is a challenge.

- **Communication Overhead**: The overhead of network communication between services can impact performance.

Building and Deploying Microservices with Spring Boot

Spring Boot is an ideal framework for building microservices, as it provides an easy way to create standalone, production-grade applications that can be deployed with minimal configuration. Spring Boot simplifies the process of building microservices by providing auto-configuration, embedded servers (such as Tomcat or Jetty), and the Spring Cloud suite for distributed systems.

Steps to Build a Microservice with Spring Boot:

1. **Set Up Spring Boot**:
    - ᴜ Create a new Spring Boot application using **Spring Initializr** (https://start.spring.io/) or directly from your IDE (e.g., IntelliJ IDEA or Eclipse).
    - ᴏ Select the necessary dependencies such as **Spring Web**, **Spring Boot DevTools**, and **Spring Data JPA** for database integration.

2. **Create Microservice Components**:

o Each microservice should have its own set of business logic, controllers, and models. In this example, we will build a simple e-commerce system with services for **Product Management** and **Order Management**.

3. **Service Layer**: Implement business logic in the service layer. Each microservice should expose a set of RESTful APIs for communication with other services or clients.

   o **Example of Product Microservice (`ProductService.java`)**:

```java
@Service
public class ProductService {

    private final ProductRepository productRepository;

    @Autowired
    public ProductService(ProductRepository productRepository) {
        this.productRepository = productRepository;
    }
```

```java
    public              List<Product>
getAllProducts() {
        return
productRepository.findAll();
    }

    public                   Product
getProductById(Long id) {
        return
productRepository.findById(id).orEl
seThrow(()            ->           new
ResourceNotFoundException("Product
not found"));
    }

    public                   Product
addProduct(Product product) {
        return
productRepository.save(product);
    }
}
```

o **Product   Controller**
   (`ProductController.java`):

java

```java
@RestController
@RequestMapping("/api/products")
public class ProductController {
```

265

```java
    private    final    ProductService
productService;

    @Autowired
    public
ProductController(ProductService
productService) {
        this.productService        =
productService;
    }

    @GetMapping
    public              List<Product>
getAllProducts() {
        return
productService.getAllProducts();
    }

    @GetMapping("/{id}")
    public                    Product
getProductById(@PathVariable    Long
id) {
        return
productService.getProductById(id);
    }

    @PostMapping
```

```
public                  Product
addProduct(@RequestBody      Product
product) {
        return
productService.addProduct(product);
    }
}
```

4. **Database Integration**: Each microservice should have its own database (or schema). Spring Data JPA or JDBC can be used to interact with databases.

5. **Deploying Microservices**:
   o After building the microservices, you can deploy them using Docker, Kubernetes, or directly to cloud platforms such as **AWS**, **Azure**, or **Google Cloud**.

   o **Run the Application**: To run your Spring Boot microservices locally:

   ```bash
   ```

   ```
   mvn spring-boot:run
   ```

API Gateway and Service Discovery

In a microservices architecture, managing communication between services can become complex. To address this, we use an **API Gateway** and **Service Discovery**.

267

API Gateway:

The **API Gateway** is a server that acts as a single entry point for all clients to access microservices. It routes client requests to the appropriate microservice, handles load balancing, and can also handle cross-cutting concerns like authentication, logging, and rate limiting.

- **Spring Cloud Gateway** is a popular API Gateway solution that works seamlessly with Spring Boot microservices.

  Example of Configuring Spring Cloud Gateway:

  java

```java
@SpringBootApplication
@EnableDiscoveryClient
public class GatewayApplication {

    public static void main(String[] args)
{

SpringApplication.run(GatewayApplication.
class, args);
    }

    @Bean
```

```
    public                RouteLocator
customRouteLocator(RouteLocatorBuilder
builder) {
        return builder.routes()
            .route("product_service", r ->
r.path("/api/products/**")
                .uri("lb://PRODUCT-
SERVICE"))
                .route("order_service",  r  ->
r.path("/api/orders/**")
                .uri("lb://ORDER-
SERVICE"))
            .build();
    }
}
```

- o This code defines routes for two microservices
  (Product-Service and Order-Service)
  using Spring Cloud Gateway.

Service Discovery:

Service Discovery allows microservices to dynamically discover each other without hardcoding URLs. **Eureka** (from Spring Cloud) and **Consul** are popular service discovery tools.

- **Spring Cloud Netflix Eureka** is commonly used for service discovery. Microservices register themselves with

Eureka, and the API Gateway can query Eureka to find the available services.

- o **Example of Enabling Eureka in Spring Boot**:

```java
@SpringBootApplication
@EnableEurekaServer
public class EurekaApplication {

    public static void main(String[]
args) {

SpringApplication.run(EurekaApplica
tion.class, args);
    }
}
```

- o The `@EnableEurekaServer` annotation turns your application into a **Eureka Server** where microservices can register.

Real-World Example: Developing a Microservice-based E-Commerce System

Let's put everything together by building a **simple microservice-based e-commerce system**. This system will have two main services:

1. **Product Service**: Manages products.
2. **Order Service**: Manages customer orders.

Step 1: Create the Product Service

The **Product Service** microservice will handle CRUD operations for products.

- `ProductService` and `ProductController` were already outlined earlier. This service allows customers to add and view products.

Step 2: Create the Order Service

The **Order Service** will handle customer orders and their interaction with products.

```java
@RestController
@RequestMapping("/api/orders")
public class OrderController {

    private final ProductService productService;

    @Autowired
    public      OrderController(ProductService
productService) {
        this.productService = productService;
```

271

```
    }


    @PostMapping
    public     Order     placeOrder(@RequestBody
OrderRequest orderRequest) {
        Product          product          =
productService.getProductById(orderRequest.getP
roductId());
        Order   order   =   new   Order(product,
orderRequest.getQuantity());
        // Save the order to the database (in a
real system)
        return order;
    }
}
```

Step 3: Integrating with the API Gateway and Service Discovery

1. **API Gateway**: As discussed, configure the API Gateway to route requests to both the Product Service and Order Service.

2. **Service Discovery**: Use **Eureka** to register the services.

- Each microservice registers itself with Eureka, and the API Gateway uses service names (e.g., PRODUCT-SERVICE) to route requests dynamically.

Step 4: Deploying the Microservices to the Cloud

1. **Dockerize the Microservices**: Create Dockerfiles for both the Product Service and Order Service.
2. **Deploy with Kubernetes or Cloud Providers**: Deploy the microservices using **AWS**, **Google Cloud**, or **Azure**, or orchestrate them using **Kubernetes**.

Conclusion

In this chapter, we explored **microservices architecture** and how to build, deploy, and manage Java-based microservices using **Spring Boot**. We discussed the concepts of **API Gateway**, **Service Discovery**, and how these tools enable efficient communication between services. A real-world example of a **microservice-based e-commerce system** demonstrated how to develop and integrate microservices for a complete application. In the next chapter, we will delve into **advanced microservices topics**, such as managing distributed transactions, securing microservices, and monitoring performance.

CHAPTER 21

SECURITY IN JAVA APPLICATIONS

In this chapter, we will discuss the essential aspects of **securing Java applications**. We will examine some of the most common **security vulnerabilities** found in Java applications, including **SQL Injection, Cross-Site Scripting (XSS)**, and **Cross-Site Request Forgery (CSRF)**. We will then move on to **secure coding practices** and the use of the **Java Security API** to protect applications from these vulnerabilities. Additionally, we will cover **authentication** and **authorization**, focusing on best practices. Finally, we will implement a **real-world example** of **OAuth2 authentication** in a Java application.

Common Security Vulnerabilities (SQL Injection, XSS, CSRF)

Java applications, like all software systems, are susceptible to security vulnerabilities. Understanding these common vulnerabilities and knowing how to prevent them is crucial in building secure applications.

SQL Injection (SQLi):

SQL Injection occurs when a malicious user can manipulate an SQL query by injecting arbitrary SQL code into an application's input fields, potentially leading to unauthorized access or data manipulation.

- **Example of SQL Injection**:

```java
java
```

```java
String query = "SELECT * FROM users WHERE
username = '" + username + "' AND password
= '" + password + "'";
Statement              stmt              =
connection.createStatement();
ResultSet rs = stmt.executeQuery(query);
```

In this example, if `username` or `password` contain malicious input, such as:

```sql
sql
```

```sql
' OR 1=1 --
```

This would allow attackers to bypass authentication and potentially retrieve all users from the database.

- **Prevention**:

- o Use **Prepared Statements** with **parameterized queries**:

```java
String query = "SELECT * FROM users
WHERE username = ? AND password = ?";
PreparedStatement        pstmt        =
connection.prepareStatement(query);
pstmt.setString(1, username);
pstmt.setString(2, password);
ResultSet rs = pstmt.executeQuery();
```

Cross-Site Scripting (XSS):

XSS vulnerabilities allow attackers to inject malicious scripts into web pages viewed by other users. These scripts can steal user data or perform actions on behalf of the user.

- **Types of XSS**:
  - o **Stored XSS**: Malicious script is stored on the server and executed when other users view the affected page.
  - o **Reflected XSS**: Malicious script is reflected off the server in the response.
- **Example of XSS**:

```html
```

```
<div>
    <h1>Welcome, ${username}!</h1>
</div>
```

If the `username` contains a script tag:

html

```
<script>alert('XSS Attack!');</script>
```

This could execute the script in the browser.

- **Prevention**:
    - **Escape HTML output**: Use Java's `StringEscapeUtils` or **JSP/Thymeleaf** to properly escape user-generated content.
    - **Use Content Security Policy (CSP)**: CSP restricts the sources from which scripts can be loaded.

Cross-Site Request Forgery (CSRF):

CSRF exploits the trust that a web application has in the user's browser. An attacker tricks a user into making an unwanted request, such as transferring funds or changing account details, without the user's consent.

- **Example of CSRF**: An attacker could send a request from a different site that triggers an action in the target application, e.g., transferring money:

```
html
```

```
<img
src="http://example.com/transfer?amount=1
000&to=attacker" />
```

- **Prevention**:
  - **Use Anti-CSRF tokens**: Always include a random token in forms and validate it server-side.
  - **SameSite Cookies**: Set cookies with `SameSite` attribute to prevent them from being sent along with cross-site requests.

Secure Coding Practices and Java Security API

Following secure coding practices is essential to protect Java applications from common vulnerabilities. The **Java Security API** provides a set of classes for encryption, authentication, and access control.

Secure Coding Practices:

1. **Input Validation**:

278

- o Always validate and sanitize input to prevent malicious data from entering your system.
- o Use **whitelists** (acceptable patterns) for input validation instead of **blacklists**.

2. **Data Encryption**:

- o Always encrypt sensitive data, both in transit and at rest.
- o Use strong encryption algorithms like **AES** and **RSA**.
- o **Example**: Using `Cipher` to encrypt data:

```java
Cipher cipher =
Cipher.getInstance("AES");
SecretKeySpec key = new
SecretKeySpec("1234567890123456".ge
tBytes(), "AES");
cipher.init(Cipher.ENCRYPT_MODE,
key);
byte[] encrypted =
cipher.doFinal(data.getBytes());
```

3. **Use HTTPS**:

- o Ensure that communication between clients and servers is encrypted using **SSL/TLS** (HTTPS).

4. **Exception Handling**:

279

- o Avoid exposing stack traces or sensitive information in error messages.
- o Use proper logging mechanisms to track errors securely.

Java Security API:

The **Java Security API** provides classes for:

- **Cryptography**: `MessageDigest`, `Cipher`, `KeyPairGenerator`, etc.
- **Authentication and Authorization**: `Principal`, `Permissions`, `AccessControlManager`.
- **Digital Signatures**: `Signature`, `PublicKey`, `PrivateKey`.

Example of using the **MessageDigest** class to hash passwords:

java

```
MessageDigest md = MessageDigest.getInstance("SHA-256");
byte[] hash = md.digest(password.getBytes(StandardCharsets.UTF_8));
String hashedPassword = bytesToHex(hash);
```

Authentication and Authorization

Authentication verifies who the user is, and **Authorization** determines what the user can do.

Authentication:

Authentication is the process of verifying the identity of a user. Common methods include:

- **Basic Authentication**: User credentials are sent with every request (insecure unless over HTTPS).
- **Token-Based Authentication**: Modern systems use tokens like **JWT (JSON Web Tokens)** for stateless authentication.
- **OAuth2**: A widely used framework for authentication and authorization. OAuth2 allows third-party services to access user data without sharing credentials (for example, logging in with Google or Facebook).

Authorization:

Authorization checks if an authenticated user has permission to access a specific resource or perform an action. Common methods include:

- **Role-based Access Control (RBAC)**: Assigning roles to users and restricting access based on roles.

- **Attribute-based Access Control (ABAC)**: Granting access based on attributes like user location, device, or time of access.

Real-World Example: Implementing OAuth2 Authentication in a Java Application

OAuth2 is commonly used to allow users to authenticate through third-party providers (e.g., Google, Facebook, etc.). In this example, we will implement **OAuth2 authentication** in a Java Spring Boot application to authenticate users using Google.

Step 1: Set Up Spring Security and OAuth2:

Add the necessary dependencies to your `pom.xml` for Spring Security and OAuth2:

xml

```xml
<dependency>
    <groupId>org.springframework.boot</groupId>
    <artifactId>spring-boot-starter-oauth2-
client</artifactId>
</dependency>
```

Step 2: Configure Application Properties:

In the `application.yml` (or `application.properties`), configure the OAuth2 client with your Google OAuth2 credentials.

```yaml
spring:
  security:
    oauth2:
      client:
        registration:
          google:
            client-id: YOUR_GOOGLE_CLIENT_ID
            client-secret:
YOUR_GOOGLE_CLIENT_SECRET
            scope: profile, email
            authorization-grant-type:
authorization_code
            redirect-uri:
"{baseUrl}/login/oauth2/code/{registrationId}"
        provider:
          google:
            authorization-uri:
https://accounts.google.com/o/oauth2/auth
            token-uri:
https://oauth2.googleapis.com/token
```

```
      user-info-uri:
https://www.googleapis.com/oauth2/v3/userinfo
```

Step 3: Implement OAuth2 Login:

Spring Boot automatically configures OAuth2 login with the Google provider using the configuration from `application.yml`.

- **Login with Google**: When users access the application, they are redirected to the Google login page. Upon successful authentication, they are redirected back to the application with an OAuth2 token.

Step 4: Securing Access to Resources:

Use **Spring Security** to restrict access to authenticated users. For example, you can protect a resource like `/dashboard`:

```java
@Configuration
@EnableWebSecurity
public class SecurityConfig extends
WebSecurityConfigurerAdapter {

    @Override
    protected void configure(HttpSecurity http)
throws Exception {
        http
```

```
        .authorizeRequests()
        .antMatchers("/",
"/login").permitAll()

.antMatchers("/dashboard").authenticated()
        .and()
        .oauth2Login();
    }
}
```

Step 5: Access User Information:

Once the user is authenticated, you can access their details using the OAuth2AuthenticationToken:

```
java

@GetMapping("/dashboard")
public String dashboard(@AuthenticationPrincipal
OAuth2User principal) {
    String            userName            =
principal.getAttribute("name");
    return "Hello, " + userName;
}
```

Conclusion

In this chapter, we explored **security in Java applications**, focusing on common vulnerabilities like **SQL Injection**, **XSS**, and **CSRF**, and how to prevent them. We also covered **secure coding practices**, the **Java Security API**, and the concepts of **authentication** and **authorization**. Finally, we demonstrated how to implement **OAuth2 authentication** in a Java application using **Spring Security** to authenticate users via Google. By implementing strong security measures, you can ensure your Java applications are protected from common attacks and secure user data. In the next chapter, we will explore **performance optimization** techniques for Java applications.

CHAPTER 22

JAVA FOR BIG DATA AND HADOOP

In this chapter, we will dive into the world of **Big Data** and explore how Java can be used to process and analyze large datasets using tools like **Hadoop** and **Apache Spark**. Big Data refers to the massive volume of data that traditional data processing applications are unable to handle efficiently. We will explore key concepts in Big Data, the Java APIs for **Hadoop** and **Spark**, and how Java can be used for **distributed computing**. To make things concrete, we'll finish the chapter with a **real-world example** of processing large datasets using **Hadoop**.

Introduction to Big Data Concepts

Big Data refers to datasets that are too large or complex to be processed by traditional data processing tools, such as relational databases or spreadsheets. Big Data is often characterized by the **3 Vs**:

1. **Volume**: The sheer amount of data being generated every second (e.g., social media posts, sensor data, etc.).

2. **Velocity**: The speed at which data is generated and needs to be processed (e.g., real-time data streams).

3. **Variety**: The different types and formats of data (e.g., structured, unstructured, and semi-structured data).

Big Data applications require specialized frameworks for storage, processing, and analysis. Two of the most widely used frameworks for Big Data processing are **Hadoop** and **Apache Spark**.

Hadoop:

Hadoop is an open-source framework for storing and processing large datasets in a distributed computing environment. It provides two main components:

1. **Hadoop Distributed File System (HDFS)**: A distributed storage system that stores data across multiple machines.

2. **MapReduce**: A programming model and processing engine for processing large datasets in parallel across many machines.

Apache Spark:

Apache Spark is a fast, in-memory, distributed computing framework that builds on Hadoop's MapReduce. It is widely used for batch processing and real-time data processing. Spark provides libraries for SQL, machine learning, graph processing, and streaming.

Java APIs for Hadoop and Spark

Java is widely used in the Big Data ecosystem, and both **Hadoop** and **Spark** provide Java APIs to interact with their systems.

Hadoop Java API:

The **Hadoop Java API** allows Java developers to write programs that interact with the Hadoop Distributed File System (HDFS) and perform **MapReduce** jobs. Here's a quick overview of key components:

- **HDFS API**: For interacting with Hadoop's file system (e.g., reading and writing files).
- **MapReduce API**: For writing distributed data processing programs using the MapReduce programming model.

Example of Reading and Writing to HDFS in Java:

```java

import org.apache.hadoop.fs.*;
import org.apache.hadoop.conf.*;

public class HDFSExample {
```

```java
    public static void main(String[] args) throws
Exception {
        Configuration      conf      =      new
Configuration();
        FileSystem fs = FileSystem.get(conf);

        Path        path        =        new
Path("/user/hadoop/input.txt");
        FSDataInputStream      inputStream      =
fs.open(path);

        // Read file
        String line;
        while ((line = inputStream.readLine())
!= null) {
            System.out.println(line);
        }
        inputStream.close();

        // Write file
        Path        outputPath        =        new
Path("/user/hadoop/output.txt");
        FSDataOutputStream      outputStream      =
fs.create(outputPath);
        outputStream.write("Hello
Hadoop!".getBytes());
        outputStream.close();
    }
}
```

- In the above example, we read data from a file stored in HDFS and write data to another file.

Apache Spark Java API:

Apache Spark provides a Java API to interact with its in-memory processing engine. The core abstraction in Spark is the **RDD (Resilient Distributed Dataset)**, which represents a distributed collection of objects. Java developers can use Spark's API to perform operations like filtering, grouping, and reducing data in parallel across a cluster.

Example of Processing Data with Apache Spark in Java:

java

```
import org.apache.spark.api.java.*;
import org.apache.spark.SparkConf;
import
org.apache.spark.api.java.function.Function;
import java.util.List;

public class SparkExample {
    public static void main(String[] args) {
        SparkConf        conf        =        new
SparkConf().setAppName("Java           Spark
Example").setMaster("local");
        JavaSparkContext      sc      =      new
JavaSparkContext(conf);
```

```java
        // Create an RDD from a list
        List<String> data = List.of("apple",
"banana", "cherry", "date");
        JavaRDD<String>         rdd         =
sc.parallelize(data);

        // Perform transformation (filter out
fruits with 'a')
        JavaRDD<String>       filteredRdd     =
rdd.filter(new Function<String, Boolean>() {
            @Override
            public Boolean call(String fruit) {
                return fruit.contains("a");
            }
        });

        // Collect and print the result
        List<String>          filteredData    =
filteredRdd.collect();

filteredData.forEach(System.out::println);

        sc.close();
    }
}
```

- In this example, we filter out fruits that contain the letter "a" using **JavaSparkContext** and the **RDD** API.

Distributed Computing with Java

Distributed computing refers to the use of multiple machines to solve a problem in parallel. Both **Hadoop** and **Apache Spark** enable distributed computing by dividing tasks into smaller sub-tasks and processing them across multiple nodes in a cluster.

Hadoop Distributed Computing:

- **MapReduce** splits the input data into chunks, processes them in parallel across a cluster of machines, and aggregates the results.
- **HDFS** allows data to be stored across multiple machines, making it fault-tolerant and enabling distributed computation.

Apache Spark Distributed Computing:

- **RDDs** are the fundamental data structure in Spark and enable distributed processing.
- Spark performs computations in parallel across multiple nodes using its **in-memory** processing engine, which is faster than Hadoop MapReduce for certain tasks.

In both Hadoop and Spark, Java is used to write programs that can process data in parallel across multiple nodes, leading to faster computations and the ability to handle large datasets.

Real-World Example: Processing Large Datasets with Hadoop

Now, let's walk through a real-world example of how we can use **Hadoop** to process large datasets. We will write a simple **MapReduce** program in Java that calculates the **word count** of a large text file.

Step 1: Setting Up the Hadoop Environment:

- Install **Hadoop** on a single-node or multi-node cluster.
- Configure the Hadoop environment variables and paths (e.g., HADOOP_HOME, HDFS, JAVA_HOME).

Step 2: Write the Mapper and Reducer Classes:

1. **Mapper Class**: This class processes the input data and outputs key-value pairs (e.g., word, 1).

```java
import org.apache.hadoop.io.*;
import org.apache.hadoop.mapreduce.*;

import java.io.IOException;

public class WordCountMapper extends
Mapper<LongWritable, Text, Text, IntWritable> {
```

294

```java
    private Text word = new Text();
    private final static IntWritable one = new
IntWritable(1);

    @Override
    public void map(LongWritable key, Text value,
Context        context)        throws        IOException,
InterruptedException {
        String[]                words                =
value.toString().split("\\s+");
        for (String w : words) {
            word.set(w);
            context.write(word, one);
        }
    }
}
```

2. **Reducer Class**: This class aggregates the results from the Mapper and calculates the total count for each word.

```java
java

import org.apache.hadoop.io.*;
import org.apache.hadoop.mapreduce.*;

import java.io.IOException;

public class WordCountReducer extends
Reducer<Text, IntWritable, Text, IntWritable> {
```

295

```java
    private  final  IntWritable  result  =  new
IntWritable();

    @Override
    public        void        reduce(Text        key,
Iterable<IntWritable>  values,  Context  context)
throws IOException, InterruptedException {
        int sum = 0;
        for (IntWritable val : values) {
            sum += val.get();
        }
        result.set(sum);
        context.write(key, result);
    }
}
```

Step 3: Driver Class:

The **Driver Class** configures and runs the MapReduce job.

java

```java
import org.apache.hadoop.conf.*;
import org.apache.hadoop.fs.*;
import org.apache.hadoop.io.*;
import org.apache.hadoop.mapreduce.*;

public class WordCount {
```

```java
    public static void main(String[] args) throws
Exception {
        Configuration    conf    =    new
Configuration();
        Job  job  =  Job.getInstance(conf,  "word
count");

        job.setJarByClass(WordCount.class);

job.setMapperClass(WordCountMapper.class);

job.setReducerClass(WordCountReducer.class);

        job.setOutputKeyClass(Text.class);

job.setOutputValueClass(IntWritable.class);

        FileInputFormat.addInputPath(job,    new
Path(args[0]));
        FileOutputFormat.setOutputPath(job,    new
Path(args[1]));

        System.exit(job.waitForCompletion(true)
? 0 : 1);
    }
}
```

Step 4: Running the Job:

Once the code is ready, you can run the Hadoop job with the following commands:

1. Upload the input file to HDFS:

```bash
hdfs dfs -put input.txt /user/hadoop/input
```

2. Run the Hadoop job:

```bash
hadoop   jar   WordCount.jar   WordCount
/user/hadoop/input /user/hadoop/output
```

3. Retrieve the results:

```bash
hdfs dfs -cat /user/hadoop/output/part-r-
00000
```

Conclusion

In this chapter, we explored **Big Data** concepts and how **Java** can be used to process large datasets using tools like **Hadoop** and

Apache Spark. We discussed key components of Hadoop, including **HDFS** and **MapReduce**, and demonstrated how to write a simple **MapReduce program** in Java for word counting. We also saw how Java can be used for **distributed computing** with tools like Hadoop and Spark, enabling efficient processing of massive datasets across multiple machines. In the next chapter, we will explore **Java for machine learning** and the integration of Java with machine learning libraries.

CHAPTER 23

JAVA FOR MOBILE DEVELOPMENT (ANDROID BASICS)

In this chapter, we will explore **Android development** using **Java**. Android is the most widely used mobile operating system, and Java remains one of the primary languages for developing Android applications. We will walk through the basics of Android development, set up the necessary development environment, and build a simple **To-Do List app** to demonstrate how Java is used in Android app development.

Introduction to Android Development with Java

Android is an open-source operating system primarily used for mobile devices like smartphones, tablets, and wearables. It is based on the **Linux kernel** and provides a rich application framework for building mobile apps.

- **Java** is the most commonly used programming language for Android development, though Kotlin has become popular recently as well.

- **Android SDK**: The Android Software Development Kit (SDK) provides a comprehensive set of tools, libraries, and APIs that enable you to develop, test, and deploy Android applications.

Key Concepts in Android Development:

- **Activity**: An activity is a single screen in your app with which users can interact. It's the main entry point for an app.
- **View**: A UI element (button, text field, image, etc.) that can be displayed on the screen.
- **Layout**: A container for views, determining how they are arranged on the screen.
- **Intent**: A messaging object that allows app components to request actions from other components (like opening a new screen or starting a service).

Setting Up Android Studio

To begin Android development, you need to install **Android Studio**, the official integrated development environment (IDE) for Android development.

Step 1: Install Android Studio

1. **Download Android Studio**:

- o Visit the official Android Studio website and download the installer for your operating system.

2. **Install Android Studio**:
   - o Follow the installation instructions for your OS (Windows, macOS, or Linux).
   - o The installation includes the **Android SDK**, **Android Emulator**, and **necessary tools**.

Step 2: Configure Android Studio

- **Install SDK Packages**: During the setup, Android Studio will prompt you to install additional SDK packages, including essential libraries and Android APIs.
- **Create an Android Virtual Device (AVD)**: The Android Emulator allows you to run and test your Android apps on a virtual device, mimicking a real phone or tablet.

Step 3: Set Up Your Android Project

Once Android Studio is installed and configured, you can start a new project:

1. **Open Android Studio** and select **Start a New Android Studio Project**.
2. **Choose Project Template**:
   - o For beginners, **Empty Activity** is a good starting point.
3. **Configure Your Project**:

- o   Name your app (e.g., "ToDoListApp").
- o   Select the language (**Java**) and set the **minimum API level** (choose an API level that supports most devices, typically **API 21+**).
4. **Click Finish** to create the project.

Android Studio will automatically generate the basic project structure, which includes:

- **MainActivity.java**: The main activity of your app.
- **activity_main.xml**: The layout file that defines how the UI looks.

Building Your First Android Application

Now that you've set up Android Studio, let's build your first Android app: a simple **To-Do List app**. This app will allow users to add tasks, view them in a list, and delete tasks.

Step 1: Design the User Interface (UI)

The UI for the **To-Do List app** will include:

- A **TextView** for displaying the title.
- An **EditText** for entering new tasks.
- A **Button** for adding tasks to the list.
- A **ListView** for displaying the tasks.

Here's how you can design the layout in `activity_main.xml`:

xml

```xml
<?xml version="1.0" encoding="utf-8"?>
<LinearLayout
xmlns:android="http://schemas.android.com/apk/r
es/android"
    android:layout_width="match_parent"
    android:layout_height="match_parent"
    android:orientation="vertical"
    android:padding="16dp">

    <TextView
        android:id="@+id/textViewTitle"
        android:layout_width="wrap_content
```

You said:

Chapter 24: Reactive Programming with Java • Introduction to Reactive Programming Concepts • Using Project Reactor and RxJava • Building Asynchronous Applications • Real-World Example: Real-Time Data Stream Processing System

ChatGPT said:

Chapter 24: Reactive Programming with Java

In this chapter, we will explore **Reactive Programming** and how it can be used to build **asynchronous, event-driven applications** in Java. Reactive programming is a paradigm that allows developers to handle asynchronous data streams in a more functional and declarative way. We will cover key concepts of **Reactive Programming**, introduce two of the most popular libraries for reactive programming in Java—**Project Reactor** and **RxJava**—and then apply these concepts to create a **real-time data stream processing system**.

Introduction to Reactive Programming Concepts

Reactive Programming is a programming paradigm focused on handling asynchronous events and data streams. It allows systems to react to changes in data or events, and it can be highly useful for building scalable, real-time applications.

Core Principles of Reactive Programming:

1. **Asynchronous**: Reactive programming focuses on non-blocking, asynchronous processing. This allows for better performance and scalability, especially in systems with many I/O-bound operations.
2. **Event-driven**: The flow of data in a reactive system is driven by events. When an event occurs, the system reacts to it by processing or transforming the data associated with the event.
3. **Streams**: Data is treated as streams, and you can apply various operators to these streams. A stream represents a

305

sequence of asynchronous data that can be observed and transformed.

4. **Backpressure**: Reactive systems should be able to handle cases where the rate of data production exceeds the rate at which data can be processed (e.g., preventing out-of-memory errors).

5. **Declarative**: You describe how the system should react to changes in data, rather than defining the detailed steps of how it reacts.

Reactive Streams:

The **Reactive Streams API** defines a standard for asynchronous stream processing in Java. It includes the concepts of **Publisher, Subscriber, Subscription**, and **Processor**. Libraries like **Project Reactor** and **RxJava** implement this API.

Using Project Reactor and RxJava

Both **Project Reactor** and **RxJava** are popular libraries that facilitate reactive programming in Java. They provide rich APIs for dealing with asynchronous streams, including operators for filtering, transforming, and combining streams.

Project Reactor:

Project Reactor is a reactive library built on top of the **Reactive Streams** specification. It is a part of the **Spring Framework** and is widely used in **Spring WebFlux** for building reactive web applications.

- **Mono**: A **Mono** represents a sequence of 0 or 1 item.
- **Flux**: A **Flux** represents a sequence of 0 to N items.

Example of creating a simple **Mono** and **Flux** in Reactor:

java

```java
import reactor.core.publisher.Mono;
import reactor.core.publisher.Flux;

public class ReactorExample {
    public static void main(String[] args) {
        // Creating a Mono that emits a single value
        Mono<String> mono = Mono.just("Hello, Reactive!");
        mono.subscribe(System.out::println);

        // Creating a Flux that emits multiple values
        Flux<Integer> flux = Flux.range(1, 5);
        flux.subscribe(System.out::println);
```

```
    }
}
```

In this example:

- **Mono.just** creates a Mono that emits a single value.
- **Flux.range** creates a Flux that emits a sequence of integers.

RxJava:

RxJava is another popular library for reactive programming, inspired by **Reactive Extensions (Rx)**. It supports functional programming concepts and operators like **map, flatMap, filter, and combineLatest**.

Example of creating an observable and subscriber in RxJava:

java

```java
import io.reactivex.rxjava3.core.Observable;

public class RxJavaExample {
    public static void main(String[] args) {
        // Create an Observable that emits items
        Observable<String>     observable     =
Observable.just("Hello", "Reactive", "World");

        // Subscribe to the Observable
```

```
observable.subscribe(
        item                                  ->
System.out.println("Received: " + item),
        throwable                             ->
System.err.println("Error: " + throwable),
        () -> System.out.println("Done")
    );
  }
}
```

In this example:

- **Observable.just** creates an Observable that emits a list of items.
- **subscribe** allows you to define what to do when an item is emitted, when an error occurs, and when the sequence completes.

Building Asynchronous Applications

One of the primary use cases of **Reactive Programming** is building **asynchronous applications** that handle large volumes of events or data streams without blocking the main execution thread. This is particularly useful for handling I/O-bound operations, like HTTP requests or database queries.

Asynchronous Processing with Project Reactor:

To demonstrate how to handle asynchronous tasks in Project Reactor, let's create a simple application where a task (e.g., fetching data from an API or performing some computation) runs asynchronously, and the main thread continues with other operations.

Example of asynchronous data processing using Reactor:

```java
import reactor.core.publisher.Mono;

public class AsynchronousExample {
    public static void main(String[] args) throws
InterruptedException {
        // Simulating an asynchronous task
        Mono<String>           asyncTask           =
Mono.fromCallable(() -> {
            Thread.sleep(1000);
            return "Task Completed!";
        });

        // Non-blocking subscription
        asyncTask.subscribe(result            ->
System.out.println("Received: " + result));

        // Main thread continues processing
```

310

```
        System.out.println("Main           thread
continues without blocking");

        // Sleep to allow async task to complete
before the application exits
        Thread.sleep(1500);
    }
}
```

- In this example, the task is executed asynchronously using `Mono.fromCallable()`, and the main thread is not blocked while waiting for the task to complete.

Asynchronous Processing with RxJava:

With RxJava, asynchronous processing can be done by using the **observeOn** and **subscribeOn** operators, which allow you to specify the thread for the observable to run on and where the subscription should be executed.

```java
import io.reactivex.rxjava3.core.Observable;

public class AsynchronousRxJavaExample {
    public static void main(String[] args) throws
InterruptedException {
        // Simulating an asynchronous task with
RxJava
```

311

```
        Observable<String>        observable      =
Observable.create(emitter -> {
        Thread.sleep(1000);
        emitter.onNext("Task Completed!");
        emitter.onComplete();
    });


    // Subscribe on a background thread and
observe the result on the main thread
        observable
        .subscribeOn(Schedulers.io())      //
Running task in background
        .observeOn(Schedulers.single())    //
Observing on a single thread
        .subscribe(result                  ->
System.out.println("Received: " + result));


    // Main thread continues without blocking
        System.out.println("Main          thread
continues without blocking");


    // Sleep to allow async task to complete
before the application exits
        Thread.sleep(1500);
    }
}
```

Real-World Example: Real-Time Data Stream Processing System

Let's now build a **real-time data stream processing system** using **Project Reactor**. The system will simulate processing streaming data, such as sensor readings or stock prices, and apply transformations like filtering and aggregating data.

Step 1: Simulating a Real-Time Data Stream

We'll create a Flux that generates random data (e.g., stock prices) every second.

```java
import reactor.core.publisher.Flux;
import java.time.Duration;

public class RealTimeStreamExample {
    public static void main(String[] args) {
        // Simulating real-time stock price data stream
        Flux<Double>     stockPriceStream     =
Flux.interval(Duration.ofSeconds(1))
            .map(i -> Math.random() * 100)   // Generate random stock prices
            .take(10);  // Limit to 10 prices

        stockPriceStream.subscribe(price -> {
```

```
        System.out.println("Received    stock
price: " + price);
    });

    // Sleep to allow data stream processing
    try {
        Thread.sleep(12000); // Sleep to let
stream complete
    } catch (InterruptedException e) {
        e.printStackTrace();
    }
    }
}
```

Step 2: Transforming and Aggregating Data

Now, let's apply some transformations to the stream, such as filtering out prices above a certain threshold and calculating the average price.

java

```
import reactor.core.publisher.Flux;

public class RealTimeStreamProcessing {
    public static void main(String[] args) {
        Flux<Double>      stockPriceStream      =
Flux.interval(Duration.ofSeconds(1))
            .map(i -> Math.random() * 100)
            .take(10)
```

```
        .filter(price -> price > 50)    //
Filter out prices less than 50
        .doOnNext(price                 ->
System.out.println("Filtered  stock  price:  " +
price));

        // Calculate the average of the filtered
stock prices
        stockPriceStream.collectList()
        .map(prices                     ->
prices.stream().mapToDouble(Double::doubleValue
).average().orElse(0))
        .subscribe(avgPrice             ->
System.out.println("Average  stock  price:  " +
avgPrice));

        // Sleep to allow data processing
        try {
            Thread.sleep(12000);  // Sleep to let
stream complete
        } catch (InterruptedException e) {
            e.printStackTrace();
        }
    }
}
```

In this example:

- We simulate stock price data.
- We filter out prices below 50.

315

- We calculate the average of the remaining stock prices.

Conclusion

In this chapter, we introduced **Reactive Programming** in Java and demonstrated how to use **Project Reactor** and **RxJava** to build **asynchronous, event-driven applications**. We explored key concepts such as **asynchronous data streams**, **backpressure**, and **reactive operators**. Using these tools, we built a **real-time data stream processing system** that processes and aggregates stock price data. Reactive programming offers a powerful way to handle asynchronous events and large-scale data in real-time, and is highly effective for building scalable, non-blocking applications. In the next chapter, we will dive into **advanced Java performance optimization** techniques for fine-tuning application speed and efficiency.

CHAPTER 25

PERFORMANCE OPTIMIZATION AND PROFILING IN JAVA

In this chapter, we will focus on the essential aspects of **performance optimization** in Java applications. Optimizing performance is crucial for building scalable, fast, and responsive applications. We will explore techniques for **analyzing performance bottlenecks**, using **profiling tools**, and implementing **code optimization strategies**. Finally, we will walk through a **real-world example** of optimizing a **Java web application** to improve its performance.

Analyzing Performance Bottlenecks

Performance bottlenecks are the parts of an application that limit its overall performance. These can occur at various levels of an application, from the database layer to the user interface. Identifying and addressing bottlenecks is the first step in optimization.

Common Performance Bottlenecks:

1. **CPU-bound operations**: When an application consumes excessive CPU resources due to inefficient algorithms, tight loops, or excessive object creation.

2. **I/O-bound operations**: When an application spends too much time waiting for input/output operations like database queries, network calls, or file access.

3. **Memory consumption**: Excessive memory usage can cause the application to slow down due to frequent garbage collection or memory leaks.

4. **Thread contention**: When multiple threads compete for resources, leading to inefficient multi-threading or deadlock situations.

Analyzing Performance Bottlenecks:

To identify bottlenecks, you need to measure various aspects of the application, such as execution time, memory usage, CPU utilization, and thread behavior.

- **Application Profiling**: Profiling is the process of measuring the performance of an application at various levels to detect bottlenecks. Profilers can give you detailed insights into method execution times, memory usage, and thread behavior.

Profiling Tools and Techniques

Profiling tools are used to monitor and analyze the performance of a Java application. These tools provide valuable data to help identify performance issues.

Key Profiling Tools for Java:

1. **VisualVM**:
   - o **VisualVM** is a powerful tool for profiling Java applications. It provides real-time monitoring, memory usage analysis, and thread analysis.
   - o Features include **heap dumps, CPU profiling, memory profiling**, and **Garbage Collection (GC)** analysis.
   - o **How to use VisualVM**:
     - ▪ Download and install **VisualVM** from the official website.
     - ▪ You can attach VisualVM to a running Java process and monitor its performance.
2. **JProfiler**:
   - o **JProfiler** is a commercial profiling tool that provides in-depth analysis of Java applications, including memory, CPU, thread, and database performance.

319

o It supports real-time monitoring and can be integrated with various build tools like **Maven** and **Gradle**.

3. **YourKit**:

    o **YourKit** is another commercial profiler for Java that focuses on memory and CPU profiling, with additional tools for monitoring thread execution and garbage collection.

4. **Java Flight Recorder (JFR)**:

    o **JFR** is a tool provided by **Oracle** to collect and analyze performance metrics of Java applications. It allows for low-overhead profiling and is suitable for long-running applications.

Using VisualVM for Profiling:

- **Step 1**: Start your Java application with profiling enabled:

```bash
```

```
java                                      -
Xrunjdwp:transport=dt_socket,server=y,sus
pend=n,address=5005 -jar YourApp.jar
```

- **Step 2**: Open **VisualVM** and connect to your application running on port 5005.

- **Step 3**: Monitor CPU, memory, and thread activity. Analyze the **heap dumps** and **garbage collection logs** for performance insights.

Code Optimization Strategies

Once you've identified performance bottlenecks using profiling tools, the next step is to optimize the code. There are several strategies for improving the performance of Java applications.

1. Optimize Algorithms and Data Structures:

- Inefficient algorithms and data structures can dramatically affect performance, especially for large datasets.
- **Big O Notation**: Always consider the time and space complexity of algorithms. For example, replacing a **linear search** (`O(n)`) with a **binary search** (`O(log n)`) can significantly improve performance.
- **Choose the right data structures**: Using a **HashMap** (constant time complexity for lookups) instead of a **List** (linear time complexity for lookups) can drastically reduce execution time for certain operations.

2. Memory Management:

- **Avoid unnecessary object creation**: Excessive object creation can cause memory bloat and put pressure on the garbage collector.
- **Reuse objects**: For instance, use **StringBuilder** instead of concatenating strings in a loop.
- **Object pooling**: Use object pools for expensive-to-create objects, such as database connections or thread pools.

3. Concurrency and Threading:

- **Use thread pools**: Instead of creating new threads for each task, use thread pools to manage thread creation and avoid overhead.
- **Avoid blocking**: Use **asynchronous programming** to prevent threads from blocking on I/O operations.

4. Minimize Synchronization:

- **Minimize synchronization** on shared resources, as it can lead to thread contention. Use **java.util.concurrent** classes (like `ExecutorService` and `ConcurrentHashMap`) instead of synchronized collections.

5. Avoiding Garbage Collection Overhead:

- Frequent **garbage collection (GC)** can slow down your application. To reduce GC overhead:
    - **Reduce object allocation** and improve **object reuse**.
    - Use the **Right Garbage Collector**: The default **ParallelGC** works for most cases, but **G1GC** and **ZGC** are more efficient for large heaps and low-latency applications.

Real-World Example: Optimizing a Java Web Application for Performance

Now, let's apply these optimization strategies to a real-world scenario—optimizing a **Java web application** for performance.

Imagine you have a **simple e-commerce web application** with features like **user login**, **product search**, and **checkout**. Over time, you notice that certain operations are slow, especially during peak traffic.

Step 1: Profiling the Application

First, you use **VisualVM** or **JProfiler** to identify bottlenecks. You discover:

- **Slow product search**: The search queries are taking a long time to complete.
- **High memory usage**: The application is consuming a lot of memory during the checkout process.

Step 2: Optimizing Product Search:

- **Problem**: The current search uses a simple **linear search** over a large database.
- **Solution**: Replace the linear search with a **full-text search engine** (like **Elasticsearch** or **Apache Solr**) to improve search speed.

Step 3: Optimizing Memory Usage:

- **Problem**: The checkout process creates too many temporary objects, causing high memory usage and frequent garbage collection.
- **Solution**:
  - Reuse objects (e.g., use a **StringBuilder** for concatenating product names).
  - Optimize session management to reduce memory usage.
  - Implement **object pooling** for database connections, reducing the overhead of frequent connection creation.

324

Step 4: Improving Concurrency:

- **Problem**: During checkout, the application handles high volumes of requests and some threads are blocked.
- **Solution**:
  - Use **thread pools** to manage concurrency, avoiding the overhead of creating new threads for each request.
  - Implement **asynchronous processing** for non-blocking operations (like sending confirmation emails).

Step 5: Reducing Garbage Collection Impact:

- **Problem**: The application experiences pauses during garbage collection.
- **Solution**:
  - Optimize memory usage by reducing unnecessary object creation.
  - Use **G1 Garbage Collector** for low-latency applications to minimize GC pause times.

Step 6: Load Testing:

After implementing optimizations, perform **load testing** using tools like **Apache JMeter** or **Gatling** to simulate high traffic and ensure that the application can handle the load without performance degradation.

Conclusion

In this chapter, we explored the critical aspects of **performance optimization** in Java applications. We discussed how to **analyze performance bottlenecks** using profiling tools like **VisualVM** and **JProfiler**. We also covered several **code optimization strategies**, including improving algorithms, memory management, concurrency, and minimizing garbage collection overhead. Finally, we applied these concepts to a **real-world example** of optimizing a **Java web application** to handle high traffic and improve overall performance.

In the next chapter, we will dive into **Java for cloud-native development**, exploring how Java can be used to build and deploy applications in cloud environments using modern technologies like **containers** and **Kubernetes**.

CHAPTER 26

JAVA IN THE INTERNET OF THINGS (IOT)

In this chapter, we will explore the integration of **Java** with the **Internet of Things (IoT)**. IoT refers to the network of interconnected devices, sensors, and systems that communicate and exchange data. Java has become an important language in the development of IoT applications because of its versatility, portability, and extensive libraries. We will dive into the basics of IoT, discuss Java libraries and frameworks tailored for IoT, and examine how Java can be used to **connect devices** such as **sensors** and **actuators**. Finally, we will walk through a **real-world example** of building an **IoT-based home automation system**.

Basics of IoT and Java's Role

Internet of Things (IoT) refers to the interconnection of physical devices—**sensors**, **actuators**, **controllers**, and **gadgets**—that collect and exchange data over the internet. These devices can range from simple sensors that monitor temperature or humidity to more complex systems like smart thermostats or wearable health trackers.

Key Concepts of IoT:

1. **Devices**: These are the physical objects or sensors that collect data or interact with the environment (e.g., smart thermostats, motion sensors).

2. **Connectivity**: Devices connect to the internet using communication protocols like **Wi-Fi, Bluetooth, Zigbee,** or **LoRaWAN**.

3. **Data Processing**: The data from IoT devices is sent to **cloud platforms** or **edge devices** for processing and analysis.

4. **Actuators**: Actuators are devices that perform actions based on the data received from sensors (e.g., turning on lights, adjusting the thermostat).

Why Java for IoT?:

Java is an ideal language for IoT due to the following reasons:

- **Platform Independence**: Java runs on any platform that supports the Java Virtual Machine (JVM), making it suitable for a wide range of IoT devices.
- **Robust Ecosystem**: Java has a rich set of libraries, frameworks, and tools for communication, data processing, and device management.
- **Security**: Java provides robust security features, making it suitable for building secure IoT systems.

- **Scalability**: Java-based IoT solutions can scale from simple sensors to large, complex systems with thousands of devices.

Java Libraries and Frameworks for IoT

Several Java libraries and frameworks are specifically designed to help developers build IoT applications. These libraries facilitate communication between devices, data processing, and interaction with cloud services.

1. Eclipse IoT (Eclipse Kura, Eclipse Paho):

- **Eclipse Kura** is an IoT gateway framework that provides essential features such as device management, data collection, and protocol support.
- **Eclipse Paho** is a library for implementing **MQTT** (Message Queuing Telemetry Transport), a lightweight messaging protocol often used in IoT applications for communication between devices and servers.

2. Pi4J:

Pi4J is a popular Java library that allows Java programs to interact with the **Raspberry Pi** hardware. It provides support for GPIO (General Purpose Input/Output), sensors, and actuators on the Raspberry Pi.

- **Example**: You can use Pi4J to control LEDs or read data from a temperature sensor connected to a Raspberry Pi.

3. Java ME Embedded:

Java ME Embedded is a lightweight version of Java designed for small devices with limited resources (e.g., microcontrollers). It provides a runtime environment that can run on constrained devices, enabling developers to build IoT applications on low-power devices.

4. MQTT (Message Queuing Telemetry Transport):

- **MQTT** is a lightweight, publish/subscribe messaging protocol designed for low-bandwidth and high-latency environments, commonly used in IoT systems.
- Java clients like **Eclipse Paho** or **HiveMQ** can be used to implement MQTT communication in IoT applications.

Connecting Devices with Java (Sensors, Actuators)

IoT systems involve connecting various types of devices, sensors, and actuators to the network. Java provides the necessary tools and libraries to interface with these devices.

1. Sensors:

Sensors are devices that collect data from the environment. Examples include temperature sensors, humidity sensors, and motion sensors. In Java, sensors are typically accessed using platform-specific libraries or communication protocols like **I2C** or **SPI**.

- **Example**: Using a temperature sensor (e.g., DHT11 or DS18B20) with **Raspberry Pi** and **Pi4J** to read the temperature:

java

```java
import com.pi4j.io.gpio.*;
import com.pi4j.io.gpio.event.*;

public class TemperatureSensor {
    public static void main(String[] args) {
        // Initialize the sensor
        DHT11Sensor    sensor    =    new
DHT11Sensor(4);  // GPIO Pin 4

        // Read temperature and humidity
        sensor.read();
        System.out.println("Temperature: "
+ sensor.getTemperature() + "°C");
```

331

```java
        System.out.println("Humidity:  " +
sensor.getHumidity() + "%");
    }
}
```

2. Actuators:

Actuators are devices that perform physical actions based on commands from the IoT system. Examples include motors, lights, and switches.

- **Example**: Using Pi4J to control an LED light connected to a Raspberry Pi:

```java
java

import com.pi4j.io.gpio.*;

public class LEDControl {
    public static void main(String[] args) {
        // Create a GPIO controller
        final GpioController gpio =
GpioFactory.getInstance();

        // Provision the GPIO pin (Pin 1
for LED)
        final GpioPinDigitalOutput ledPin
=
```

```
gpio.provisionDigitalOutputPin(RaspiPin.G
PIO_01, "LED", PinState.LOW);


        // Blink the LED
        for (int i = 0; i < 10; i++) {
            ledPin.high(); // Turn LED on
            try  {   Thread.sleep(500);   }
catch (InterruptedException e) { }
            ledPin.low();  // Turn LED off
            try  {   Thread.sleep(500);   }
catch (InterruptedException e) { }
        }


        // Shutdown the GPIO controller
        gpio.shutdown();
    }
}
```

Real-World Example: Building an IoT-based Home Automation System

Let's now build a simple **IoT-based Home Automation System** using Java. In this system, we will control home appliances (e.g., lights) and monitor environmental parameters (e.g., temperature) through a mobile application or web interface.

Step 1: Set Up the System Components

1. **Raspberry Pi**: We'll use a **Raspberry Pi** as the central controller for the home automation system.
2. **Sensors**: We'll use a **DHT11 sensor** to measure the room temperature and humidity.
3. **Actuators**: We'll control an **LED** to simulate turning on/off a light.
4. **Communication**: Use **MQTT** to send commands to control the light from a remote client.

Step 2: Connect the Devices

- **Sensor (DHT11)**: Connect the DHT11 sensor to the Raspberry Pi GPIO pins.
- **Actuator (LED)**: Connect an LED to the Raspberry Pi GPIO pin.
- **MQTT Broker**: Use an MQTT broker like **Mosquitto** to facilitate communication between devices.

Step 3: Implement the Server (Raspberry Pi)

Here, we'll create a simple MQTT server that reads data from the temperature sensor and controls the light based on the incoming MQTT messages.

```java
```

```java
import org.eclipse.paho.client.mqttv3.*;

public class HomeAutomationServer {
    private static final String BROKER_URL =
"tcp://localhost:1883"; // MQTT Broker URL
    private static final String TOPIC =
"home/automation";

    public static void main(String[] args) throws
MqttException {
        MqttClient client = new
MqttClient(BROKER_URL,
MqttClient.generateClientId());
        client.connect();

        // Subscribe to the topic for controlling
the lights
        client.subscribe(TOPIC, (topic, message)
-> {
            String msg = new
String(message.getPayload());
            System.out.println("Received
command: " + msg);
            if (msg.equals("ON")) {
                // Turn on the LED
                // (Assume there's a function to
control the LED)
                turnOnLED();
            } else if (msg.equals("OFF")) {
```

```java
                // Turn off the LED
                // (Assume there's a function to
control the LED)
                turnOffLED();
            }
        });


        // Publish temperature data to the topic
        MqttMessage  temperatureMessage  =  new
MqttMessage("22.5°C".getBytes());
        client.publish("home/temperature",
temperatureMessage);


        // Run the server indefinitely
        while (true) { }
    }


    private static void turnOnLED() {
        // Logic  to  turn  on  the  LED  (GPIO
control)
        System.out.println("Turning    on    the
light.");
    }


    private static void turnOffLED() {
        // Logic  to  turn  off  the  LED  (GPIO
control)
        System.out.println("Turning    off    the
light.");
```

```
    }
}
```

Step 4: Implement the Client (Mobile/Web Interface)

You can build a mobile or web interface to send MQTT messages to control the devices. The client will send messages like "ON" or "OFF" to control the light.

```java
import org.eclipse.paho.client.mqttv3.*;

public class HomeAutomationClient {
    private static final String BROKER_URL =
"tcp://localhost:1883";
    private static final String TOPIC =
"home/automation";

    public static void main(String[] args) throws
MqttException {
        MqttClient        client        =        new
MqttClient(BROKER_URL,
MqttClient.generateClientId());
        client.connect();

        // Publish command to turn on the light
        MqttMessage        message        =        new
MqttMessage("ON".getBytes());
        client.publish(TOPIC, message);
```

337

```
    // Publish command to turn off the light
    message                =                new
MqttMessage("OFF".getBytes());
        client.publish(TOPIC, message);

        client.disconnect();
    }
}
```

Conclusion

In this chapter, we explored **Java's role in the Internet of Things (IoT)** and how it can be used to build and control IoT systems. We discussed the basics of IoT, key Java libraries for IoT, and how Java can connect sensors and actuators to build a fully functional IoT system. We walked through a **real-world example** of creating an **IoT-based home automation system** using Java, **MQTT**, and a **Raspberry Pi**. With Java's flexibility and the power of IoT frameworks, building scalable and responsive IoT applications has never been easier. In the next chapter, we will explore **Java's role in artificial intelligence and machine learning**.

CHAPTER 27

FUTURE OF JAVA AND EMERGING TRENDS

In this final chapter, we will explore the **future of Java** and the **emerging trends** that are shaping its evolution. Java has been one of the most widely used programming languages for decades, and its continued relevance in modern software development is fueled by constant updates, new features, and innovative tools. We will look at how Java is evolving, the latest trends in the Java ecosystem, and how developers can prepare for the future of Java development. Finally, we will conclude with guidance on how to **master Java for complex projects**.

Java's Evolution and New Features

Java has come a long way since its inception in 1995. Over the years, it has seen numerous improvements, both in performance and in the breadth of its ecosystem. Java is still one of the leading programming languages, mainly due to its **robustness**, **portability**, **security**, and **scalability**.

Java's Evolution:

1. **Java 5 (2004)** - Introduced **Generics, Metadata annotations**, and the **for-each loop**, which significantly enhanced Java's expressiveness.

2. **Java 7 (2011)** - Brought features like the **try-with-resources statement, diamond operator**, and **NIO 2.0** (new file I/O API).

3. **Java 8 (2014)** - A major milestone for Java, introducing **Lambda expressions, Streams API, Default methods,** and **new Date/Time API**. This version revolutionized how developers write Java code, enabling functional-style programming.

4. **Java 9 (2017)** - Introduced **modules** (Java Platform Module System), providing a way to modularize Java applications and improve application performance and security.

5. **Java 10 and 11 (2018)** - With **Java 10**, Java embraced **local-variable type inference** (using `var` keyword). **Java 11** introduced **Long-Term Support (LTS)** and various optimizations.

6. **Java 14 (2020)** - Enhanced performance and added **records** and **pattern matching** (in preview), improving code clarity and conciseness.

7. **Java 16 (2021)** - Introduced the **JEP 376** for **Unix-domain socket support** and continued improvements to **Project Loom** and **Project Panama**.

New Features in Java:

- **Records (Java 14/15)**: A new feature aimed at reducing boilerplate code when creating data-carrying classes. Records provide a concise syntax for defining immutable data types.

```java
public record Person(String name, int age)
{}
```

- **Pattern Matching (Java 16)**: Simplifies complex instanceof checks and casts. This feature improves code readability and reduces redundancy.

```java
if (obj instanceof String s) {
    // Directly use 's' as a String
}
```

- **Sealed Classes (Java 17)**: Introduced sealed classes that allow developers to control the class hierarchy and restrict which other classes can extend them, ensuring a more secure and predictable design.

```java
```

```
public sealed class Shape permits Circle,
Square { }
```

- **JEP 376: Unix Domain Socket Support** (Java 16): Improves inter-process communication, particularly useful for microservices running on Linux-based systems.

Java's evolution demonstrates its continuous adaptation to modern software engineering practices. It has incorporated features that simplify code writing (like lambda expressions and records) and provide better modularity, concurrency, and performance.

Trends in Java Development

Several emerging trends are driving the future of Java development. These trends are geared toward improving performance, scalability, and developer productivity.

1. Modularization with Project Jigsaw (Java 9):

- With the introduction of **Project Jigsaw** in Java 9, Java has embraced **modularization**. Modularization allows large applications to be broken into smaller, independent modules, making them easier to maintain, deploy, and optimize.

- It provides better control over the application's dependencies, making it easier to include or exclude parts of the system as needed. This is especially useful for large-scale enterprise applications and microservices.

2. GraalVM:

- **GraalVM** is a high-performance, embeddable virtual machine for running Java, JavaScript, Ruby, R, Python, and WebAssembly applications. It brings ahead-of-time compilation to Java, which allows Java applications to run faster with **native images**.
- GraalVM can be used to compile Java applications into **native executables**, providing faster startup times and reduced memory usage, making it ideal for microservices and serverless architectures.

Benefits of GraalVM:

  o Reduced **cold start times** for cloud-native applications.
  o Lower **memory overhead**.
  o Enhanced support for **polyglot programming**.

Example: A Java application compiled with GraalVM Native Image will run faster and consume less memory compared to running on the regular JVM.

343

3. Project Loom:

- **Project Loom** aims to simplify concurrency in Java by providing lightweight **fibers** as an alternative to threads. This allows Java applications to handle millions of concurrent tasks efficiently.
- **Fibers** are much lighter than traditional threads, making it feasible to write scalable applications with massive concurrency without the overhead associated with threads.

4. Cloud-Native Java (Microservices):

- **Java for Cloud-Native Development**: With the rise of **cloud-native** applications and **microservices architectures**, Java has become more aligned with cloud computing platforms (such as **AWS**, **Azure**, and **Google Cloud**).
- **Spring Boot** and **Spring Cloud** have become essential tools for building microservices with Java. These frameworks provide out-of-the-box solutions for handling common challenges in microservices development, such as service discovery, configuration management, and fault tolerance.
  - o **Kubernetes and Docker**: Java applications are increasingly being containerized and orchestrated using **Docker** and **Kubernetes**, enabling faster

344

deployment and scaling of Java-based microservices.

5. Reactive Programming:

- **Reactive programming** with libraries like **Project Reactor** and **RxJava** is gaining popularity for building non-blocking, event-driven systems. Reactive programming allows applications to handle large volumes of data or I/O operations asynchronously, improving performance and scalability.

6. Machine Learning and AI:

- Java has been gradually integrating with **machine learning** and **artificial intelligence** through frameworks like **Deeplearning4j**, **Weka**, and **Apache Spark MLlib**. As AI and ML become more ubiquitous, Java developers are increasingly adopting these tools for building intelligent applications.

Preparing for the Future of Java

As Java continues to evolve, developers need to stay informed and adapt to the changing landscape. Here are some strategies to prepare for the future of Java development:

1. Stay Updated with Java Releases:

Java releases are now on a **time-driven release cycle**, with new versions released every six months. Keep your skills up-to-date by learning about new features introduced in each Java release, from language features to performance improvements.

2. Embrace Modern Java Practices:

- Adopt **functional programming** techniques introduced in Java 8 and enhanced in later versions (e.g., lambda expressions, streams, and pattern matching).
- Use **Project Jigsaw** for modularization and better project structure.
- Explore **GraalVM** for compiling Java applications into native images and enhancing performance.

3. Learn Cloud and Microservices:

With Java's growing importance in cloud-native development, become proficient in tools like **Spring Boot**, **Docker**, and **Kubernetes**. Understanding **microservices architecture** and **distributed systems** is crucial as applications shift towards the cloud.

4. Master Reactive and Asynchronous Programming:

As demand for real-time applications increases, mastering **Reactive Programming** frameworks like **Project Reactor** or **RxJava** will be crucial for building scalable and efficient systems.

5. Keep an Eye on Emerging Technologies:

Stay informed about emerging trends like **GraalVM**, **Project Loom**, and the rise of **AI/ML** in Java. These innovations can significantly enhance application performance and enable developers to build smarter, more scalable applications.

Conclusion: Mastering Java for Complex Projects

Java has maintained its place as one of the most powerful, flexible, and widely used programming languages in the world. By continually evolving, Java stays relevant in the modern software development landscape, with new features that allow developers to tackle complex problems efficiently.

To master Java for complex projects, focus on the following:

1. **Mastering the language and its libraries**: Keep up with the latest Java features and libraries.
2. **Understanding modern software development paradigms**: Embrace concepts like **modularization**,

microservices, reactive programming, and cloud-native development.

3. **Leveraging powerful tools**: Use tools like **GraalVM**, **Spring Boot**, and **Project Loom** to optimize performance, improve scalability, and ensure that your applications remain fast and efficient.

By continuously learning and adapting to emerging technologies, you can leverage Java's full potential for building complex, high-performance applications for the future. The future of Java is bright, and with the right mindset and tools, you'll be well-equipped to take on any challenge.

www.ingramcontent.com/pod-product-compliance
Lightning Source LLC
LaVergne TN
LVHW051429050326
832903LV00030BD/2983